That's So Diva!

A Teen Girl's Guide to Loving Herself and Living Beautifully

Andrea K. Spoor

That's So Diva! A Teen Girl's Guide to Loving Herself and Living Beautifully
Published by Magnolia House Publishing
Greenwood Village, CO

Publisher's Cataloging-in-Publication data

Names: Spoor, Andrea Kathleen, author.
Title: That's so diva! : a teen girl's guide to loving herself and living beautifully / by Andrea Spoor.
Description: First trade paperback original edition. | Greenwood Village [Colorado] : Magnolia House Publishing, 2019. | Also published as an ebook.
Identifiers: ISBN 978-1-7329793-0-7
Subjects: LCSH: Young women—Life skills guides. | Young women—Psychology. | Young women—United States—Conduct of life. | Teenagers—Psychological aspects. | Self-esteem in adolescence.
BISAC: YOUNG ADULT NONFICTION / Inspirational & Personal Growth
Classification: LCC BF 724.3.R47 | DDC 155.533–dc22

Cover by Ali Romley
Interior design by Brianne Smith

QUANTITY PURCHASES: Schools, companies, professional groups, clubs, and other organizations may qualify for special terms when ordering quantities of this title. For information, email info@magnoliahousepublishing.com.

Contents

Dedication

To my beautiful mother who gave me life and has been
a phenomenal example of how to live empowered,
strong, loving, and kind. It is a precious gift
to be your daughter and to have had
such a wonderful mentor.
I love you, Mom.

That's So Diva!

A Teen Girl's Guide to Loving Herself and Living Beautifully

Introduction

Hello! My name is Diva, and I will be guiding you through your teenage years. I am a goddess and will be introducing you to your inner goddess. Before you know it, you will be "divafied" and ready to conquer some of the most difficult and wondrous years of your life.

So what does it really mean to be a diva? Well, I've gotten a bad rap over the years. I've heard people take my name in vain and say things like "She's *such* a diva! She thinks she's better than everyone else and the whole world revolves around her. Ugh!" They misrepresent me and misunderstand me. In fact, I don't think they are really talking about me. What they should have been saying is "She's *so* Desdemona!"

You see Desdemona is my evil sister who is fussy, super high-strung, and demanding. She tries to build a wall between your current self and your best self to block you from happiness and success. She certainly doesn't believe that the rules of kindness, compassion, and courtesy—which are diva traits—apply to her. She takes advantage of girls with low self-esteem by being the mean voice in their heads, telling them terrible things about themselves and making them believe they are not worthy enough, pretty enough, smart enough, or capable enough. She takes advantage of other girls by superficially inflating their egos, making them think they are better than everyone else, and thereby giving them permission to be cruel. She's that negative voice in your head, and she has built an army of helpers who will gladly feed that negativity. Those helpers show up as the bullies in your life, and Desdemona is their leader.

I, Diva, am the positive voice in your head and heart, leading you to places where you can use your unique beauty and gifts, and shine brightly. I'm the one who whispers possibilities in your ears, inspires you with dreams and visions, protects you with my wisdom, and stirs up excitement within you. I'm the one who reminds you that you've *so* got this, regardless of what anyone else thinks. I'm that faithful piece of you—that piece of you that "knows" you are exactly where you need to be and on the right path. I'm the one who keeps you strong and yet lovingly soft even when the world around you seems so hardened. I'm the one who inspires you to be a light in the darkness, combat hate with love, and, in a nutshell, the one who guides you on your path to your best, most joyful, and purposeful life.

I've been calling out to you all of your life, but you haven't always been listening. Maybe you think that you haven't needed me until now. Or maybe Desdemona's critical inner voice has so affected you that you haven't chosen to acknowledge me, and the positive personal wisdom I've been sharing with you. I think it's an age thing. You see, you have needed me before but not the same way you are going to need me going forward into your teenage years.

At this age, you are going through a lot of changes emotionally, physically, and socially. You are entering those years in which you are embarking on a new journey of self-discovery, which can be very confusing. You are in that awkward space where you are no longer a child, but you're not quite an adult yet either. You are becoming more independent but still need the safety net of your parents. You may even be testing some boundaries. You really are on an exciting adventure right now, even though it may seem overwhelming.

Desdemona would never reveal my true purpose and nature, so I'm going to share it with you now. My name, Diva, actually means goddess. Goddesses touch and bless the lives of others with their charisma, beauty, and unique gifts. *Every* girl has a goddess within her, and every goddess has gifts that are unique to them—attributes that make them shine, light up, and inspire those around them. You see, goddesses want the best for *everyone*, and they embrace and use their gifts to bring the best to everyone they encounter. There are many famous goddesses but too many to mention. I've written a bit about some of my best goddess friends and hope that you will acquaint yourself with them. Think about them on your journey, call on them when you get stuck, and ask yourself, "What would a goddess do?" They are sure to inspire you:

Aphrodite, the Greek goddess of love and beauty, is known for enticing people around her with feelings of love. She makes those around her feel cared for and loved and shows them what love really is in the process such as selflessness, forgiveness, compassion, and grace.

❧ Venus is also a goddess of love and beauty, but she has another gift. She is the goddess in charge of modesty. She wants you to be truly seen for the amazing, young woman you are, and she wants you to embrace your "divaness" too.

❧ Athena, the goddess of war, inspires leadership and power through wisdom, ethics, justice, and the order of civilization. She is a great visionary and has the intellectual ability to see the true nature of a situation and to develop successful strategies. She sees everything as an opportunity, which makes her a great leader and problem solver. When the teen diva collaborates with Athena, win-win outcomes are discovered and created.

❧ Demeter is the goddess of the harvest and possesses great knowledge on the best way to grow and preserve. You might think this is silly, but take some time to consider what this might mean to you as a person. Think of your life as a garden and all that you want to harvest. Demeter can show you where to plant seeds and help you pull the weeds in your garden too.

🦋   Hestia, the goddess of hearth and home, guards the fire and maintains a happy home. She centers those around her with her gentle, forgiving, and serene nature. Hestia gives them security and comfort, and she helps them to accept the truths of life with grace.

🦋   Freya is a Nordic goddess of love, beauty, health, fertility, war, wealth, divination, and magic. She is also the goddess of death. That might sound scary, but death comes in many forms. For the purpose of this book, we will look at death as letting an attitude or circumstance that isn't serving your highest divaness be put to rest. She wants you to be your best, and she will help you to let go of the negative and unproductive attitudes that are in your way. Wow! That's *so* diva, Freya! Keep us positive!

You might be wondering how these goddesses apply to you as a teenager. I mean, you're a teenager, right? Well, your teenage years are a building block for the rest of your life. These are the years when you are on a journey of self-discovery. These are the years when you will be envisioning, preparing for, and creating what you want the rest of your life to look like. My goddess friends will inspire you with their gifts, and in the process, they will help you to define your unique gifts and divaness if you consider how they might deal with a situation you may be going through. I, Diva, along with these goddess friends of mine, will help prepare you for what lies ahead. Together, we are better and stronger, and we navigate change for good. As you grow in this process and spend more time with other teen divas, you all will be coming together and doing this too.

My goddess friends and I are known to be funny but also serious. We look at things in light, humorous ways. We laugh at ourselves. We laugh with (not at) others and bring laughter to people. We shine brightly even in the darkest of situations, and we find our strength in kindness and compassion. We are *not* perfect by any means because we all possess different traits and gifts. In fact, on our own, we are perfectly imperfect, but together we are perfect because we all complement and support each other with our unique gifts.

Before you go any further, I want to say—*don't panic*! Like every girl has an inner goddess, every girl also occasionally falls under the influence of Desdemona. It's normal! Here's the thing: the minute you know how to recognize the difference between when Desdemona is influencing you, and when I am influencing you, is the minute you will be on the road to making better choices and gaining better control over your life and your happiness.

It's important for you to recognize how Desdemona's mean voice shows up in your life and how I, your inner diva's voice, shows up. Simply put, I will always help you self-instruct, and Desdemona will lead you to self-destruct. I will always encourage you and guide you to live largely, productively, successfully, lovingly, and happily. Desdemona will always try to minimize you and keep you living small.

I can already hear you. You've just said, "What*ever*! This book is encouraging me to listen to the voice in my head that already makes me feel like a crazy person. This book is stupid." Well, this is a good start then. You see this is a sign that Desdemona's mean voice already inhabits your mind, and she has convinced you that you are defeated and that nothing could possibly take you out of your miseries. She has convinced you that this is as good as it will ever get for you. That's *her* speaking! She is trying to abolish any chance of you becoming your best self, and you are already buying into her nonsense. That's so *not* diva!

Here are some ways to know when Desdemona is influencing you:

◊ You are experiencing a lot of drama.

◊ You are procrastinating.

◊ You are anxious, fearful, self-loathing, and full of self-doubt.

◊ You are overly critical of yourself and others.

◊ You find yourself making excuses for why things are not possible; you are being pessimistic instead of optimistic.

◊ You are not taking ownership of your actions and inactions.

◊ You are having trouble with your friends and family.

◊ You are constantly looking for someone or something to blame rather than for solutions.

When I am influencing you:

◊ You will be focused on solutions.

◊ You will experience minimal drama.

◊ You will be energized and productive.

◊ You will feel confident.

◊ You will have a healthy self-esteem.

◊ You will feel optimistic.

◊ You will see opportunities in every situation.

◊ You will have strong and healthy relationships.

◊ You will enthusiastically own who you are and who you want to become.

Now that you have had your first lesson in deciphering the difference between Desdemona's influence and mine, I must ask: are you willing to listen to me and take me with you on your journey? I promise to be your constant companion, guiding you, and giving you the tools you need to ignore Desdemona. I will never leave your side as long as you want me by your side and open your heart and mind to listen to me.

WWADD?:
What would a diva do?

WWAGD?:
What would a goddess do?

Divaness:
Unique goddess gifts and style

Divafied:
Transformed into the amazing diva you are meant to be

About This Book

In an effort to beat Desdemona at her game, I've decided to develop my own language. You will see acronyms and diva words throughout this book. You will also see "dantras" and "power phrases" to inspire you. Read the words, memorize the dantras, and make them a part of your everyday language. They are sure to make you smile and fill you up with some diva joy. They will encourage you to be your best, which, by the way, is "divamazing!" Lastly, you will be challenged occasionally with a "Double Diva Dare Ya." I won't force you to do anything; I mean that would be so *not* diva. I want you to consider and think through the possibilities. I want you to see that even though things might really stink at times, possibilities always abound.

To get the most out of this book, be sure to write in your diva journal. Think of your journal as your best friend and secret keeper. You might be surprised at the answers you find simply by writing out your thoughts, feelings, and dreams. And, you will discover how inspiring and wise you truly are. You are *so* diva!

URSD:
You are so diva

Divamazing:
Amazing in your unique diva style

A Heartfelt Letter from Your Inner Diva

My darling teen diva,

Before you begin this journey with me, I want you to know how much I truly love you. I love you *so* much that I want you to have it all, and I want to give you your all—whatever "all" means to you—because it means something different to everyone. I want to give you everything that will help you achieve your all and make your heart sing, your eyes twinkle, and your body dance and thrive. I want to give you wings so you can fly freely with purpose. Most of all, I want to give you the gift of loving and respecting yourself. I want you to see yourself through my eyes and not through the eyes of Desdemona and her outside influences. I want you to embrace *your* unique beauty and gifts and believe in your worth. I love you so much that I want you to be free to develop into the diva you are meant to be, and I want to give you the tools to do so.

I want you to have the wisdom to realize that to have it all, you must be willing to let go of certain things to create space for your all. For you to be your best self and create your brightest future, I want you to let go of the following things:

◊ Excuses. They are nothing more than a crutch and will keep you stuck. Challenge your excuses so you can move beyond feeling like a victim and instead become a victor in your life.

◊ Living small. To live largely you have to let go of the attitudes, beliefs, and everything else that keeps you living small.

◊ Control of others. You only have control over yourself.

◊ Negativity. Your power will be found in positivity.

◊ Past experiences and the mistakes you've made. If you don't forgive yourself and let go of past mistakes, they will dictate your future and keep you stuck. Learn from them and grow, but let go of self-punishment and self-loathing.

◊ Judgment of yourself and others. Practice forgiveness, compassion, and understanding instead.

◊ Envy, jealousy, and desire for what others have. Instead, practice an attitude of gratitude, and love what you have been given and the endless opportunities that are ahead of you. If you are living in envy and jealousy, you are robbing yourself of the present moment and the beauty in everything that is a gift in *your* life right now.

◊ The negative perceptions and stories you tell yourself. Challenge yourself to let go of focusing on what's wrong and instead focus on the positives.

I want you to live confidently and self-assured, knowing you are enough in every way. You are smart enough, pretty enough, good enough, and worthy of living happily.

I want you to be confident and feel empowered to define who you are, what beauty and success mean to you, what you want, and where you want to go. Nobody else can define you or your life because they don't know you like *you* know you.

I want you to have a healthy self-image and wear your body, character, and values like a diva badge of honor because you were created perfectly beautiful, spirited, and unique.

I want to give you the gift of power behind your choices, and I want you to understand that you have the power to choose how you show up every minute of every day. Choices are constructive when made for the right reasons and destructive when made for the wrong reasons; you get to *choose* whether or not to self-instruct or self-destruct. I want you to be clear and stand strong in what is right for you and not make choices that mislead you on your path. I want you to know that if you do make choices that throw you off course, I am always here and ready to guide you back.

I want to give you the gift of living with integrity and being accountable for your actions and inactions. Living with integrity involves doing what is right, no matter who is or isn't watching, and with a joyful heart. I want you to have the tools to hold yourself to high ethical standards and have the strength to exercise integrity every day. When you are intentional and practice integrity, you will pass tested moments with flying colors.

I want to give you the tools to attract and hold on to supportive people in your life who will cheer you on your way and comfort you if you should fall. People who will celebrate your successes and support you when things don't go the way you want. People who will dream with you, motivate you, and keep you accountable to what you say you are going to do. People who see how perfect you are—as you are right now—and encourage you to continually learn and grow. People who want the best for you and help you to show up well in your life.

I want to give you the tools you need to live passionately and give 100 percent, not out of obligation but out of the desire to be a contributor and a part of solutions. I want to give you the ability to see a problem as an opportunity and, rather than complain about it, judge, and look for blame, become a great leader and focus on solutions. I want you to be the example of the light you want to see in the world and to step fully into being that light.

I want to give you the gift of compassion. You will come across people who act unkind and unlovable. I want you to have the wisdom, courage, and compassion to be kind and love them anyway because they have a story that brought them to where they are, and they probably need to be shown love and kindness the most. Be the example of love that they may never have been shown. I want you to remember that kindness and compassion are strengths, not weaknesses.

I want you to dream beautiful dreams and know the possibilities that those dreams hold for you. I want you to know that every dream is within reach as long as you are willing to allow your greatness to be seen and be courageous enough to act on your dreams. I want you to always follow your dreams and never allow the roadblocks, or the people who put them there, to stop you. Know that there is always a way to move around them and achieve anything you want.

I want to give you the gift of being fully present and experiencing the "now" moment. The past is past and cannot be changed. The future is yet to be seen and can only be written by being present in the here and now. Know that every minute you spend fully present and in the now moment affects and becomes your future. Live blissfully and presently, sweet diva! For when you are in your bliss, you are honoring your inner diva most highly and living your best life.

I want you to love yourself as much as I love you. I want you to see yourself through my eyes because all I see in you is pure beauty, love, and beautiful purpose. I want you to feel the power in writing your own story and hold that pen confidently. This world needs your beauty, gifts, presence, and unique purpose. It longs for you to confidently let the light within you shine. Everything wonderful is waiting for you with open arms, sweet girl! You are supported. Call on me whenever you need me.

With all my deepest diva love,

Diva

Chapter 1

Power Tools for the Teen Diva

The Power of Ownership

Taking ownership of your "all" and how you contribute to your all by the choices you make is the first step in becoming "response-able" and embracing your inner diva. That's so diva!

—Diva

S weet teen diva, this is a *big* one! If you don't exercise responsibility and ownership, then the other tools and guidance in this book will not be as effective. To become the person you want to become and achieve the things you want to achieve, you have to be willing to own who you are right now, the experiences that brought you to where you are right now, and how you contributed to those experiences without any big *but*s. When I talk about experiences, I am referring to successes, (perceived) failures, conflicts, mistakes, and wins. Some experiences we don't choose, such as bullying, illness, harassment, abuse, or loss of some kind. However, most other experiences we do choose. Own them, think about how they have added to your life story, and allow them to guide you positively in writing your future story.

You see, no matter what you do or what you are going through, there are pieces of you that make your experiences true for you.

Let's keep things positive. I want you to think about a success you have had. Remember, success can come in many forms, such as a good grade, a winning shot in a sporting event, a resolution in a conflict, a positive conversation with your parents, or finally getting asked out by that person you've been dying to date. Now, I want you to ask yourself, "What was it about me that contributed to the win and made it successful?" Was it your wisdom? Was it your attitude? Was it your compassion? Was it your ability to set some boundaries? Was it a personal gift or talent within you? Was it a combination of many things?

There are pieces of you that contribute to every outcome. Always keep those in mind. When you realize what piece of you contributed to the outcome, you know what to continue doing if that piece created success and what to change next time to create a different outcome if you are not happy. When you acknowledge the pieces of you that are creating your experiences, you will have the power within you to change your experiences if you so desire.

When Desdemona is influencing your ability to exercise ownership, you will
- ◊   be full of big buts—"But if they hadn't done that I ...,"
- ◊   feel guilty and ashamed like you want to hide,
- ◊   feel lazy and unmotivated,
- ◊   set expectations for others that you don't set for yourself,
- ◊   ask others to do things you wouldn't do yourself, and
- ◊   feel a lot of drama.

When I, Diva, am influencing your ability to be accountable you will feel
- ◊   calm and confident,
- ◊   optimistic,
- ◊   minimal drama, and

3

◊   totally okay owning your part in things because you know that information is valuable. The reason something didn't work is super powerful because it tells you what needs to change, so it works next time and creates success for your future.

Journal It!

- *Think of an experience you recently had that was positive and successful. What part of you contributed to the win?*
- *Think of an experience you recently had that you wish would have turned out differently. What would you do differently next time to make it a win?*

Dantra

To be able to respond effectively to the events in my life, I will own how I contributed to them.

Permission Slip

I, your inner diva, give you full permission to be accountable and own your experiences so you can create great successes and become the amazing diva you are meant to be.

Double Diva Dare Ya!

To think of something that didn't work well for you and come up with a plan to create a new and successful outcome.

The Power of Confidence and Self-Esteem

Oh, my diva! I want that kind of magnetic attraction!

—Diva

I want so much for you, sweet teen diva, and at the top of my list of wants for you is to be confident and have a healthy self-esteem. Why is this so important? Because how you feel about yourself is in direct alignment with how confidently you show up in the world—your ability to lead and inspire, your ability to have healthy relationships, and your likelihood for achieving your goals and dreams. Confidence and self-esteem go hand in hand.

So what is confidence? Have you ever been around certain people and thought, *O-M-D! I wish I could be more confident like them!* What is it about those people that makes us say, "Oh, my diva!"? Well, confidence is a feeling that you create inside of you and it radiates out to others making them feel great and inspired in your presence. Truly confident people live with integrity and have a common belief in the importance of honor and respect for everyone. Confidence is that knowing voice inside of you (your inner diva!) that says, "I've so got this!" and moves you to respect and inspire others in the process. You can choose to build your confidence by practicing new attitudes and ways of being. Let's start by exploring the attitudes of confident and esteemed teen divas:

- ◊ They have a magical way of speaking; their word is their wand.
- ◊ They are great listeners.
- ◊ They ask for help when they need it.
- ◊ They have contagiously positive attitudes.
- ◊ They are courageous.
- ◊ They love helping others succeed.
- ◊ They find the golden nugget in every experience, even experiences that most would find negative.
- ◊ They are natural problem-solvers and seek solutions that create a win-win for all.
- ◊ They are inspiring and always make those around them feel comfortable, important, and good about themselves in their presence.
- ◊ They see the glass as half full, and if they can't see the glass as half full (we are all human; it happens), they fully own it and ask for a crazy straw.
- ◊ They take a *sincere* interest in others.
- ◊ They embrace their gifts *and* their weaknesses.
- ◊ They have boundaries and use their voice.
- ◊ They take the initiative.
- ◊ They stand up to what is wrong and do what is right.
- ◊ They are humble.

◊ They are patient.

◊ They are polite.

◊ They take ownership of who they are and who they want to become.

◊ They are complimentary of others. Criticism and judgment do not fit a diva's way of being.

◊ Even when they experience a loss, they see it as a win by looking for the lesson or opportunity, so that they can create future successes.

◊ They don't compare themselves to others because they know that everyone is different and has a unique gift to bring to the table.

◊ They have a "we" attitude instead of a "me" attitude. They don't make everything about them.

◊ Super important! Confident teen divas know that when others show up hateful, critical, rude, bullish, and/ or judgmental, it has nothing to do with them. The confident and esteemed teen diva doesn't judge or get defensive. She totally gets it that the other person has a story that brought them to a place of negativity, and she sends them a genuine wish for happiness and continues to set a positive example for others.

To build on your confidence and self-esteem, start by becoming aware of the statements you make and the judgment behind them. Remember that your word is your wand. There is *big* magic in the way you talk. How you speak impacts how you make others feel, and it says a lot about how you feel about yourself. Take a look at the following chart for some examples.

Healthy Self-Esteem and Confidence	Unhealthy Self-Esteem and Confidence
Wow, that could have gone better, but now I know what I would do differently next time to improve. It's all good!	I suck at this! I'm too stupid to do this! I quit!
You totally rocked it today! Congrats!	You did well today, but if it hadn't been for Stacy having your back, things wouldn't have been so great for you, would they?
I'm really excited about my win today!	Ha-ha! I totally made the others look like losers!
Shelly looks really good today!	Shelly looks pretty good today, but I think her shoes look kinda dorky with that dress.

Sweet diva, as you move forward working on your confidence and self-esteem, keep in mind how you speak, how often you feel the need to cut someone else down, and how you make those around you feel. Consider for a minute Cady in the movie *Mean Girls*. She found great wisdom in that calling someone stupid doesn't make you smarter. Calling someone fat doesn't make you thinner. Calling someone ugly doesn't make you more beautiful. And judging someone's weaknesses won't make you stronger or a winner. None of these attitudes will win healthy friendships, relationships, or a promising future. In fact, they might cost you friendships and opportunities. When you make people feel good about themselves, you will feel great about yourself and become a magnet to many wonderful things in life. The more positive experiences you allow yourself to have by being positive and inspiring, the more confidence you will gain.

Combined with your character, confidence and self-esteem are key to achieving what you want and preparing yourself for your future. I want you to know that *everyone* has confidence and self-esteem within them, but some have had it weakened or buried by their experiences. Others have had it stifled by the messages or labels that make them feel like they are not "enough" in some way. As a confident and esteemed teen diva, I encourage you to pay those individuals a *big* diva compliment and remind them that they are enough and *more*.

Desdemona might be influencing your confidence and self-esteem if
 ◊   you are being pessimistic,
 ◊   you are critical or judgmental of yourself or others,
 ◊   you are getting into a lot of trouble,
 ◊   you are being disrespectful,
 ◊   you are mean-spirited,
 ◊   you are full of self-doubt,
 ◊   you live by negative labels that outside influences gave you, or
 ◊   you wish badly for others so you can win.

9

These are ways to combat Desdemona when she tries to stifle your confidence and self-esteem:

◊ Pay someone a compliment every day.

◊ Perform an anonymous random act of kindness.

◊ Offer to lend a helping hand to someone who is struggling.

◊ Take an interest in people and their stories. Make sure to exercise loyalty and don't share his or her stories with anyone else.

◊ Propose a solution to a problem you see in the community.

◊ Switch up your routine. Desdemona will get thrown off because she likes to keep people stuck in a rut.

◊ Offer to cook dinner for your mom, dad, sibling, or a friend.

◊ Call someone you haven't spoken to in a long time to let the person know you were thinking of him or her.

◊ Send someone a handwritten note that expresses gratitude for how he or she contributes to your life and makes you a better person.

◊ Do something charitable.

◊ Do something nice for *yourself*—you're worth it!

◊ Start a new kind of gossip trend: positive gossip! Brag about someone else to others.

Journal It!

- *What's one thing you can do to step outside of your comfort zone and exercise and/or stretch your confidence and self-esteem?*
- *How did you make others feel as a result?*
- *How did you feel about yourself as a result?*

Dantra

I choose to stand in my confidence, so I can live my best life and positively impact and inspire those around me to do the same—fearlessly.

Permission Slip

I, your inner diva, give you full permission to feel good about yourself and show up confidently in your life so you can have it all.

Double Diva Dare Ya!

To step outside of your comfort zone and do something to exercise your confidence.

OMD!:

Oh, my diva!

MWIMW:

My word is my wand

The Power of Choice

The choices you make today will influence the experiences you have tomorrow. But tomorrow brings new opportunities to make new and better choices that will change your experiences with every new day that follows.

—Diva

Choices! Choices! Choices! Diva darling, you make choices every day that you are fully aware of, such as what to wear, how to do your hair, and what to eat. You choose your friends, how you spend your time, the social media sites you visit, and the activities you participate in. Yet there are so many other choices that you might not realize you have available to you, such as your values, beliefs, attitude, and character. The most important choice you consciously can make each and every day is how you want to show up in the world.

As a teen diva, there are things you don't get to choose, such as going to school, doing chores, keeping your curfew, and cleaning your room when your parents ask you. If you rebel against these things, you are, without realizing it, creating and *choosing* conflict, drama, and trouble. Let me give you another example. If you don't study hard for a test and receive an unsatisfactory grade, by choosing not to study hard, you actually chose the grade you received. See how this works? Choice is crazy powerful! It can be productive and create great success, or it can be destructive and create drama and stress. The choice is yours!

Now let's flip this negative Nelly card over and talk about the power of making positive choices to arrive at an outcome you will be happy with. The key to making positive choices is to take a step back and get a clear picture of the end result you desire. Begin with the end in mind: the big picture. Think of the worst possible outcomes as well as the best possible outcomes. Consider the unintended consequences and who/what else will be impacted by your choice. Consider why you want this end result and how it will serve your greatest good. Consider how you want to feel about the end result and about yourself based on the choice you make. Why do you want to feel that way? How do you want others to feel as a result of your choice? Why do you want others to feel that way? Consider the things that you need to change in your attitude to create the desired outcome. Consider what making this choice today will mean for you tomorrow, next month, next year, and in the future. Consider if making that choice is worth the impact it could make on your future.

While some choices are easy to make, others are more difficult—especially during these years when you are stepping into more independence and exposed to more influences. The good news is that when you are aware of the things that influence you and your attitude, you have the power to choose differently and create positive outcomes. More to come on influence later.

13

When Desdemona is influencing your choices, you will feel
- ◊ twisted up in your gut like a bad feeling,
- ◊ full of "what ifs,"
- ◊ anxious,
- ◊ resentful,
- ◊ scared,
- ◊ out of balance emotionally,
- ◊ defensive,
- ◊ like you are not being totally honest with yourself or anyone else, and
- ◊ like you have to figure out how you will explain yourself or justify why you did what you did.

When you are listening to me, your inner diva, directing you to good choices, you will feel
- ◊ excited,
- ◊ balanced,
- ◊ happy and optimistic,
- ◊ like you want to share the news with everyone—(Eeks!!),
- ◊ 100 percent confident and fearless, and
- ◊ like there is nothing that will hold you back.

Journal It!

I want you to think about all of the areas of your life—your friendships, schoolwork, family, and extracurricular activities.

- *What conflicts or struggles come up as you think about these areas?*
- *What are those experiences trying to teach you?*
- *In what ways are you choosing things that bring you a negative outcome or create drama in your life?*
- *In what ways can you choose differently to create a more positive and empowered outcome while reducing stress and drama?*
- *In what areas of your life are you choosing positive outcomes?*
- *Are you choosing things that lead you to self-instruct or things that cause you to self-destruct? Why?*

Dantra

Making good choices is an exercise in confidence. I am a DITCH—a diva in total control of herself. I am completely in control of the choices I make. I understand the power behind my choices and the impact they have on others and me. I will courageously choose things that are healthy for me, are respectful to others, and in my best interest because
I am worth it!

Permission Slip

I, your inner diva, give you full permission to make choices that will feed your life in the most positive and beautiful ways because I love you and want a successful future for you.

Double Diva Dare Ya!

To stand confidently in your greatness and make more empowered choices this week. Journal how things changed for you. Was there less conflict? Did you get a better grade? Did you perform better in extracurricular activities?

DITCH:

Diva in total control of herself

When you struggle to make a choice, consult your diva!

D   Define the problem or situation. What's really going on? How did you contribute to the problem or situation? How did others contribute? What is the common thread? Is there something you need to forgive? Is there something you need to be forgiven for?

I   Inventory the options, alternatives, consequences, possible outcomes, risks, rewards, what's at stake, who will be affected. Consider the positives and negatives of each, and then weigh what's most important to you.

V   Vision and values. Picture your ideal image of the outcome you desire. Picture it in a way that creates a win-win for everyone. Then consider how to make this decision, so it is in line with your values to create victory.

    Example: If compassion is a value for you, consider how to solve the problem and make a decision compassionately with understanding and objectivity, and without judgment.

A   Act; make a decision! Do it confidently and courageously, knowing you have weighed all of the options and have done your best to create a win-win outcome.

Character is Everything!

Character is a lot easier to maintain than it is to regain!

—Diva

My dear, there are so many things I want you to understand that are hugely important, and character is among the top concepts. How you choose to show up every day and deal with your problems, dramas, successes, and conflicts, and how well you treat others tells the world a lot about your character, morals, and values. Your character will grow, change, and evolve over time and, along with a dose of confidence, will help you attract what you want in life.

Unfortunately, character can also push others away and limit your opportunities if you do not exercise positive and healthy character. Have you ever known someone who comes across super aggressively? You know, a girl who will manipulate, cheat, lie to, and stomp on anyone who gets in her way? Or a girl who is so hypercritical of herself and everyone around her that she only points out what's wrong and nothing that's right? Or perhaps you know a girl who stomps out of a room because she didn't get her way instead of hanging in to resolve a conflict. What do those attitudes reveal about their character, morals, and values? Do you think they make friends easily or have opportunities pounding down their door? Of course not! Nobody wants to be at the receiving end of deception and drama—and we divas are *drama queen dropouts!*

When you exercise positive character, you are living and staying true to who you are, your morals and values. Your morals and values are standards and behaviors that are most important to you and say the most about you. For example, if you value honesty, you probably don't lie to or for others, and you choose friends whom you can trust. If you value trust, you are probably trustworthy and honor confidence when it is asked of you.

Let me tell you a story. Ashley was at a party and found herself really bothered by another girl, Danielle, who was making fun of a friend of hers who happened to have some personal challenges. Danielle made things up about her, said mean things, and started rumors that were not true. Ashley found herself in an awkward situation because she didn't want to contribute to the conversation and didn't find anything about it funny, yet she felt stuck having to listen. Eventually, Ashley spoke up and asked Danielle why she was being so mean and how she benefited from making fun of people. Danielle responded, "Because she's a loser, and it's funny." Ashley was upset and started wondering what Danielle said behind *her* back when she wasn't around.

When Ashley got home later that evening, she couldn't get Danielle's cruelty out of her head. She felt sick about how mean she had been and worried about her friend and the impact this might have on her if the rumors spread. In that moment, Ashley made the powerful choice to "weed her garden" and stop hanging around with Danielle and the other girls who participated. Ashley realized that the gift in this situation was that she became aware of how important loyalty and true friendship were to her. She went into her heart and practiced an attitude of gratitude, and she thanked her inner diva for showing her what she never wanted to be and how she never wanted to treat people. This simple observation helped her make an empowered choice: to spend time with friends who matched her values of kindness, compassion, and trust.

Sweetheart, I want you to be observant of those around you and make empowered choices to spend time in places and with people that positively strengthen your character. If people ask you to lie for them, they will probably lie to you. If someone talks poorly behind someone else's back, he or she will most likely talk poorly behind yours too. If someone tells someone else's secrets, that person will probably tell yours too. How people behave reveals a lot about their character. Be careful with whom you choose to spend your time and what you choose to share with certain people. Make those choices based on what you value most. As you observe the behaviors of those around you, be mindful of your behaviors too. Walk your talk, sweet one!

Realize that it can be easy to fall under the influence of others and their characteristics and values (or non-values). Pssst ... here's the secret! Character and everything that contributes to your character such as values, morals, friendships, and beliefs are *choices* that you are in total control of. Make a conscious choice to surround yourself with people who match you and your values, who lift you up, whom you can trust, and who bring out your best character traits.

Create Your Character—It's a Choice!

Positive character: Look at the list below and circle the positive characteristics and values that describe who you are and who you wish to become.

Affectionate	Creative	Grateful	Loyal	Responsible
Amazing	Curious	Happy	Meticulous	Silly
Angelic	Dreamy	Helpful	Modest	Sincere
Athletic	Eager	Honest	Mysterious	Starlike
Bold	Elegant	Honorable	Open-minded	Studious
Brave	Empathetic	Hopeful	Optimistic	Stylish
Calm	Energetic	Humorous	Outgoing	Sweet
Candid	Expressive	Intelligent	Patient	Sympathetic
Clever	Fair	Jolly	Peaceful	Talented
Comfortable	Feisty	Joyful	Persistent	Thoughtful
Compassionate	Flirty	Kind	Playful	Trusting
Confident	Focused	Light-hearted	Punctual	Trustworthy
Conscientious	Forgiving	Likable	Quiet	Truthful
Considerate	Friendly	Lively	Radiant	Unselfish
Cooperative	Fun-loving	Logical	Resourceful	Warm
Courageous	Funny	Lovable	Respectful	Wise
Courteous	Generous	Loving	Risk-taking	Zany

Journal It!

- *What are the things you love the most about your character right now?*
- *Are the choices you are making in line with your ideal character and your values?*
- *In what ways does your character make you shine like a teen diva?*
- *In what ways does Desdemona influence your character? How can you counter her and develop a more positive character?*
- *What part of your character do you want to develop? In what ways can you challenge yourself to build that character?*

Dantra

My character says a lot about who I am and what I attract. I choose to live true to my values and develop a character that is positive and sets the stage to live a beautiful and purposeful life.

Permission Slip

I, your inner diva, give you full permission to choose and develop a character that will allow you to step fully and confidently into a bright future, attracting many opportunities.
BYOC!

Double Diva Dare Ya!

To choose at least one and up to three positive characteristics on your list and exercise them mindfully in all situations this week. Be aware of how it makes a difference for you and those around you.

BYOC!

Be your own character!

The Power of Your Voice

Your story cannot be written and told until you find
your voice and the courage within to use it.

—Diva

Diva darling, did you know you have a voice? Your voice is super powerful and speaks loudly about who you are, what you value, what you want, what you don't want, your character, your boundaries, your ability to solve problems, and your ability to lead and inspire. More importantly, your voice is like a shield and protects the most important parts of you: your character, your self-worth, and your dignity. How you use your voice impacts how you experience life. Your voice is a powerful tool in writing your life story.

When used effectively, your voice can create magic in your life. It can protect you, propel you forward, and get you unstuck from whatever it is that hurts or distracts you. Your voice can open up doors for you, bring you many opportunities, and help you maintain good relationships. Unfortunately, your voice can also create a lot of drama in your life when it's used ineffectively or not used at all. Yuck! Here's the thing: you can choose how to use your voice to reduce the drama in your life, create and maintain good relationships, create great successes, and protect your most valuable assets—your character and self-worth.

Sometimes it can be hard to speak up and use your voice. It can be really scary because you don't know how others will respond, or maybe you fear being judged. It can be especially frightening when you feel threatened and made to feel like you can't speak up and are left feeling completely powerless. But the sooner you address something that is hurting you, the less suffering you will endure. The sooner you speak up, the sooner you regain your power. There might be times in your life when you find yourself hurt by someone or some event. There might be times in your life when you feel disrespected or harassed. There might be times in your life when you witness someone else being hurt or disrespected. You may even find yourself feeling strongly about a cause and want to speak out and educate others to influence change. The key is to remember that you can make a difference. You do not have to suffer or watch others suffer in the process. You can choose to exercise your voice and be a vessel for change. You can choose to use your voice to make what is wrong right again. You can use your voice to lead and inspire so you can impact change in your life, your community, and the lives of others.

Using your voice is an excellent exercise in courage, confidence, and self-esteem. When used well, it says a lot about what you value most, and how you value yourself and the people and opportunities that surround you. We were given voices for a reason—to use them! Your voice is incredibly powerful. It's one of your five senses, and each sense serves you, guides you, and protects you in some way. Your voice will protect you and perhaps someone else. Don't hesitate to use it. Don't let yourself be stifled or silenced by fear, people, or situations. Let your voice set you free to live well!

Follow these diva tips on using your voice:

◊ Exercise your self-worth and speak up for yourself and others.

◊ Speak with purpose.

◊ If something is happening to you or someone else that you know isn't right, speak up!

◊ If you see something that can be improved, changed, or solved, speak up!

◊ If you see an opportunity to show compassion and care, use your voice.

◊ If you see an opportunity to inspire, use your voice.

◊ Offer to be a helping hand and share ideas about what is possible. It will speak volumes about you and your ability to lead and inspire.

◊ When you use your voice, remember that to achieve what you want, you must be aware of the tact, tone, and intent behind your voice to be effective.

◊ Voices and words can be powerful and constructive or powerfully destructive. When the teen diva uses her voice, she is all-powerful and constructive. She is inspiring!

◊ Use a power phrase—"Not today, Desdemona! I am worthy of being heard, and I've so got this!"

When Desdemona is influencing your voice, you will feel

◊ stifled,

◊ shut down,

◊ unworthy of being heard,

◊ unhappy,

- ◊ not good enough,
- ◊ threatened,
- ◊ hopeless,
- ◊ powerless,
- ◊ disrespected, and
- ◊ fearful.

When I, your inner diva, am guiding you to use your voice, you will feel

- ◊ fearless,
- ◊ powerful,
- ◊ impactful,
- ◊ inspiring,
- ◊ courageous,
- ◊ safe,
- ◊ worthy,
- ◊ strong, and
- ◊ heard.

Journal It!

Exercise your voice. Write about something you are passionate about and want to be a vessel for positive change. Speak. Be heard. Inspire!

Dantra

My voice is designed to shield and protect me and also to lead and inspire others. I choose to use my voice, be heard, and inspire those around me.

Permission Slip

I, your inner diva, give you full permission to be heard.

Double Diva Dare Ya!

To self-instruct and speak up!

Power Phrases—Developing Your Inner Diva Voice

The voice inside your mind telling you that you can't can only be silenced by the "knowing" voice in your heart (me!) telling you that you can.

—Diva

Diva darling, everyone experiences times of feeling tested in life, times of feeling "not good enough" accompanied by a fear of failing. When these feelings pop up, it's nothing more than Desdemona trying to get inside your head. In a weird and twisted way, she's trying to protect you from the pains of failure by stirring up insecurities and telling you that you're not good enough, so you won't even bother trying. But, by stopping you from trying, she's also robbing you of the possibility of success and new experiences. Gosh darn it, she's so mean, sneaky, and manipulative. The thing is that when you buy into her nonsense and don't try, you might not fail, but you will never know if you might have succeeded.

Creating a strong power phrase will help you to combat Desdemona's negativity and lies. When you are in situations that challenge you, trigger you, or stir up fear within you, you can use your power phrase to strengthen and remind yourself that—with the right attitude; a dose of confidence and self-esteem; and your bright, shining character—anything is possible.

As you begin thinking about your power phrase, consider situations that zap your confidence and how Desdemona might be influencing you and robbing you of something important. Challenge the truth of her negative voice. If you find yourself getting angry with her, it's okay. She sure makes me mad too! Let that anger empower you to create a phrase that will combat her negativity. The best way to combat her negativity is with positivity and to prove her wrong.

Now, use your unique character, language, and style to create your phrase. Be creative! The phrase should speak to your positive characteristics and be uniquely yours. For example, if you have a funny sense of humor, use that gift in your phrase. When you use your personality and unique divaness, it will become a part of you, and you will fully own it, remember it, and commit to it. Snap your fingers, wave your hands, or do something physical and sassy; then start your phrase with "Not today, Desdemona!" Try it:

◊ Not today, Desdemona! I *am* a diva, and I've *so* got this!
◊ Not today, Desdemona! I *am* a diva, and I can do this!
◊ Not today, Desdemona! I *am* a diva, and I *am* good enough!
◊ Not today, Desdemona! I *am* a diva, and I know the truth!
◊ Not today, Desdemona! I *am* a diva, and I *am* strong!
◊ Not today, Desdemona! I *am* a diva, and I *am* beautiful!
◊ Not today, Desdemona! I *am* a diva, and I *am* fearless!
◊ Not today, Desdemona! I *am* a diva, and I *am* brilliant!
◊ Not today, Desdemona! I *am* a diva, and I *am* confident!
◊ Not today, Desdemona! I *am* a diva, and this is *so* how I roll!
◊ Not today, Desdemona! I *am* a diva, and I *am* a DITCH!

Write out your power phrase, and commit to it. Use it to empower you whenever you are challenged.

My power phrase:

———————————————————————————————

———————————————————————————————

———————————————————————————————

The Teen Diva Sets Boundaries

When you don't set boundaries, you are committing yourself to being a victim of your experiences and, in the process, making an agreement with yourself that you are not worthy of what is best for you. You are a teen diva and way worthy of the best and more!

—Diva

D iva darling, setting a boundary sounds scary, right? But when you fully understand what a boundary is and what it can do for you, it won't be so scary. A boundary is a limit you set between you and someone else. Think of it as a shield designed to protect you and keep you safe in every way—emotionally, physically, and spiritually. Boundaries protect your best and highest self, and they help you stay on the right track. Setting boundaries is a huge power tool in your toolbox, an exercise in loving yourself and knowing your worth. When you don't set boundaries, you are, in a sense, committing yourself to not being worthy of what is best for you. That's so *not* diva! Learning to set boundaries is critical in building and maintaining your confidence, self-esteem, and, believe it or not, having healthy relationships.

Having boundaries means you are behaving in line with your values and beliefs. It means that you are standing in confidence and self-worth and taking responsibility for your well-being, happiness, and the things that are important to you. Boundaries are a great exercise in using your voice, and they say a lot about who you are, your character, and your values. Without boundaries you put your character at risk, and believe me when I say that character is a lot easier to maintain than it is to regain. When you respect yourself enough to set a boundary, most people in turn will show more respect for you.

Check out the examples of setting boundaries below, and you will get a better idea of what I am talking about.

1. A teen diva is working hard and feeling a tremendous amount of stress about her final exams. Her aunt stopped by and asked if she has decided on a college yet. The teen diva's response is beautiful! She said, "Auntie, thanks for taking an interest, but I'm too stressed out about my finals. Talking about college will just distract me and make it worse. When my finals are over, I'd be happy to have that conversation with you, but for now, the topic is off limits. Let's talk about it this weekend, okay?" Do you see what happened here? Setting a boundary kept her safe from distraction and stress, and it kept her focused in the moment of what was important to her. And ... she did it kindly. That's *so* diva!

2. A girl goes up to a teen diva and asks her about something they heard regarding another friend. The teen diva knows the answer because her friend confided in her, but trust is a huge value of hers, so she is not comfortable sharing. The teen diva replies, "It's really not my place to share someone else's story." This teen protected her friendship

by exercising her values of loyalty and trust, and she did it kindly but firmly. That's *so* diva!

3. A teen diva is being challenged to post something online that she knows is inappropriate and could potentially cause problems for her and someone else. Her response is "No. Why would you even ask me to do something like that when you know the damage it could cause?" What the teen diva knows in this moment is that this person doesn't have her best interest at heart. She understands the negative consequence the post could create for her. She stands confidently in her self-worth and knows she doesn't have to prove anything to anyone, especially those who clearly don't want the best for her. She knows that she will not gain anything by accepting the challenge and what accepting the challenge will *cost her*. That's *so* diva!

4. A teen diva is dating someone who asks her to do things she's uncomfortable with. He tells her that if she really cares about him, she will do it. The teen diva knows that she has the power to define when things are right for her and when they are not right for her. She doesn't allow others to pressure her. She replies, "If you really cared about me, you wouldn't put me in an uncomfortable situation and ask me to do something I don't want to do. The answer is no; I'm not ready." The teen diva says this unapologetically. She knows that mutual respect is a key to healthy relationships. That's *so* diva!

5. A teen diva has a friend who is really upset and wants her to come over right away. She was working really hard on her science project, which is due in two days. Her schedule is tight, and this is the only time she has to really focus. Her boundary is "O-M-D! I'm so sorry that happened to you! I would love to come over, but I can't tonight. Let's talk things through over the phone for a little while instead, and perhaps we can hang out tomorrow after school." This teen diva has values of loyalty, care, and compassion. Her friends are important to her, and she always wants to be supportive, but she also knows that she has to commit to her project. She sets a gentle and kind boundary while also offering an alternative that creates a win-win. That's *so* diva!

Teen divas with healthy boundaries

◊ are confident about who they are and stand on their values;

◊ know they can't control anyone else, but they can totally control themselves;

◊ speak honestly and to the point;

◊ understand that it's okay to remove themselves from people and things that go against their grain;

◊ are respectful of others;

◊ consider their options;

◊ understand that they are responsible for their own happiness; and

◊ do what is right, and stand up to what is wrong.

You might be under Desdemona's influence and need to set some boundaries if

◊ you are feeling overwhelmed and out of control,

◊ you are not feeling good about yourself,

◊ you have knots and butterflies in your tummy,

◊ you feel guilty about something you did,

◊ you allow yourself to be defined by others,

◊ you feel bullied or like people take advantage of you,

◊ you feel like your space is being invaded, or

◊ you feel off balance.

These phrases can help you set some healthy boundaries:

◊ I can't commit to that right now.

◊ No, I can't do that, but here's what I can do …

◊ I'm flattered that you asked, but I have a lot on my plate and can't do that right now.

◊ I'm *so* uncomfortable and will not do this.

◊ Stop. This isn't how I roll and doesn't work for me.

◊ No, I don't want to.

◊ This is what I need.

◊ This is hard for me to say, but …

◊ It's not my place to …, and

◊ I understand your point of view, and now I'd like you to understand mine.

Journal It!

- *What circumstances in your life give you knots and butterflies in your stomach?*
- *What are you saying yes to that you would feel better saying no to? Why?*
- *How would setting boundaries add value and create more success and balance in your life?*

Dantra

Setting a boundary is an exercise in loving myself. I choose to set boundaries kindly and respectfully, and I accept and honor the boundaries that are set with me without taking it personally.

Permission Slip

I, your inner diva, give you full permission and grant you the courage, confidence, and character to set healthy, kind, and respectful boundaries. I give you this permission because I love and respect you and know your worth.

Double Diva Dare Ya!

To pick one thing that makes you feel off balance or uneasy and set a boundary around it. Begin with the end in mind. Consider how you want to feel, how you want others to feel, and the positive change this boundary will create for you. Let me know how it goes and how things changed.

Compassion's Power

*Compassion allows you to see beyond the person, story,
or situation and into the heart without any judgment.*

—Diva

S weet diva, compassion is the ability to truly feel for other people when they are struggling and care so much that you want to help make things better—to make a difference. Lovely! After all, we divas are all about helping and supporting other divas, right? However, isn't a critical component missing from that definition? What about compassion for the self? What about caring for yourself so much that you want to feel good and do your best? Compassion for the self and compassion for others go hand in hand. To be able to have compassion for someone else, you have to be able to show compassion for yourself. I mean, you can't give what you don't have, right?

Compassion is the fuel that powers the other tools in your toolbox. It powers your confidence, self-esteem, courage, ability to set healthy boundaries, choices, and your ability to practice and exercise emotional control. Compassion is like a muscle that needs to be exercised, strengthened, and maintained. To exercise and strengthen your compassion, first acknowledge that people don't consciously choose to show up sad, upset, angry, shy, timid, mean, unkind, grumpy, bullish, or miserable. Think about it … do you know anyone who wakes up and says, "I don't need anymore happiness in my life, so I think I will choose to be a grumpy bully to anyone who crosses my path today"? Of course not! Everyone wants more happiness—even people who are really happy. But so many people have struggles that cause them, without realizing it, to act in a way that isn't ideal for them or anyone around them.

Here's the thing: Compassion is super powerful because it has the ability to completely change someone's day and perhaps his or her life. One simple act of compassion can bring hope to hopelessness, love to anger, and peace to chaos. When you can change someone's day like that, you are also changing the course of the day for yourself and everyone else. Understand that when you exercise compassion, you are exercising self-care, confidence, and self-esteem. Compassion will bring more happiness into your life and into the lives of others.

Here are some divaly ways to exercise compassion:
◊   Give a smile or a hug.
◊   Give words of encouragement.
◊   Be inquisitive.
◊   Be present.
◊   Write a caring note.
◊   Send a silent prayer or a wish.
◊   Tell someone what you admire about him or her.
◊   Imagine yourself in other people's shoes and the pain of the stories that brought them to where they are today.

◊ Offer to lend an ear to listen and a hand to help.
◊ Practice forgiveness of others and of yourself.
◊ Do something kind for someone else.
◊ Do something kind for yourself.
◊ Listen without judgment.
◊ Try to see all points of view.
◊ Carry out a random act of kindness anonymously.
◊ Be gentle with yourself and with others.
◊ Use gentle words.
◊ Don't take other people's attitudes personally.

When Desdemona is interfering with compassion, you will feel
◊ defensive,
◊ angry,
◊ hateful,
◊ mean-spirited,
◊ uncaring, or
◊ judgmental.

When I am leading you to compassion, you will feel
◊ a "knowing" inside of you that you need to do something—the right thing,
◊ a desire to help,
◊ a sense of love and concern in your heart,
◊ forgiveness,
◊ love and understanding, and/or
◊ nonjudgmental.

Journal It!

- *In what ways do you show compassion for yourself?*
- *In what ways do you show compassion for others?*
- *Think of a time when someone or some circumstance pushed your buttons.*
- *How did that person or incidence make you feel?*
- *What meaning did you attach to the incident?*
- *What or who was it about? What do you think was really going on?*
- *How would showing compassion in that incident have changed the outcome for you and others?*

Dantra

Compassion breeds happiness, light, and love and has the power to change someone's day, perhaps even his or her life and yours. I choose to give myself the gift of compassion and share that gift with others to create an atmosphere of hope and joy.

Permission Slip

I, your inner diva, give you full permission to practice and show compassion for others and yourself—and exercise positive change today.

CD4PC

Compassionate divas for positive change

41

The Power of Assertiveness

Assertiveness is the ability to go after what you want and, in the process, celebrate and respect everyone around you.

—Diva

Diva darling, practicing assertiveness will add to your confidence and help you to achieve your goals and dreams. However, I want you to understand that there is a big difference between being assertive and being aggressive. Being assertive is about going after what you want, making your dreams reality, standing up for what is right, and in the process, respecting the feelings, rights, and boundaries of others.

Aggressive girls are totally under Desdemona's spell. Even though they are actively pursuing what they want, they tend to stomp on others in the process and will do anything it takes to get what they want. Aggressive girls make others fear them—so *not* diva! Here's the thing: those girls under Desdemona's spell are losing all kinds of opportunities, such as having good friendships and support. If people are afraid of you, they will avoid you, and that is a lonely and costly place to be.

Tip: review the characteristics of confident and esteemed divas and practice those attitudes and actions as you practice assertiveness.

Assertive Teen Divas	Aggressive Desdemonas
Ask for what they want and the support they need from others, graciously	Demand and threaten to get what they want without considering others' feelings and without gratitude
Are open-minded and include others' ideas; have an optimistic attitude that anything is possible	Are controlling and closed-minded; have a "my way or the highway" attitude
Look for a win-win solution	Only care about their own win
Inspire others	Create fear within others
Make people feel comfortable	Make people feel uncomfortable
Maintain good expressions; are approachable	Are intimidating and unapproachable
Acknowledge others and give credit where credit is due	Take full credit without acknowledging others
Speak up for themselves and others respectfully	Show no respect for others and communicate harshly

Journal It!

- *Name something you are trying to achieve right now.*
- *In what ways can you practice assertiveness as you strive to reach your goals?*
- *How can you practice assertiveness in a way that is in line with your unique character, values, and beliefs?*

Dantra

I will practice assertiveness and have respect for those around me as I work to achieve my goals.

Permission Slip

I, your inner diva, give you full permission to set a positive example of assertively going after what you want in life and inspiring those around you on the way.

Double Diva Dare Ya!

To let go of any temptations to be unfair or unkind to get what you want, and instead be an inspiration and celebrate any and all outcomes.

The Power of Values

A teen diva's values are her heart's makeup.

—Diva

Values are the morals that are most important to you in your life and say the most about you. A teen diva's values are her heart's makeup. When she is living true to her values and herself, she shines beautifully, feels energized, and walks her path to purpose while making healthy choices along the way. When she isn't living true to her values, or if her values are not honored it gives her lots of answers about what she wants and doesn't want, and it empowers her to make different choices.

Your values are a big part of defining who you are and what you want in life. Your values influence how you show up every day—for your family, school, friends, and work. As long as you stay true to yourself and live by the values that are most important to you, you will continue to attract the things you want in life and stay on the right path. If you find yourself feeling lost, hurt, frustrated, or confused, check in with your values, figure out which value is not being honored, and allow yourself a little space and time to explore new choices that will bring you back into alignment with your values and back to a place of happiness.

Values are your go-to tool in every aspect of your life. They guide your choices by helping you remember what's really important to you. Take a look at the list below and circle the things that are most important to you.

Acceptance	Faith	Organization
Accomplishment	Family	Personal growth
Adventure	Flexibility	Physical fitness/health
Autonomy	Forgiveness	Power
Authenticity	Freedom	Privacy
Balance	Friendships	Quiet time
Beauty	Fun	Recognition
Commitment	Generosity	Relationships
Communication	Good grades	Reliability
Community	Happiness	Respect
Compassion	Honesty	Rest
Connecting with others	Humor	Safety
Creativity	Integrity	Self-care
Dependability	Joy	Self-expression
Determination	Kindness	Service
Education/learning	Loyalty	Spirituality
Emotional well-being	Nature	Tradition
Environment	Open-mindedness	Trust
Excellence	Optimism	Truth

Write down other values you have that might not be on the list.

_____

_____

_____

Journal It!

- *Why are the values you circled important to you?*
- *In what ways do you exercise your values?*
- *How do your values influence the choices you make?*
- *What values do you want to incorporate more into your life? List some ways to do that.*
- *In what ways do your values strengthen who you are and your identity?*

Mantra

I choose to live by and embrace my values. They say a lot about who I am, my character, and the choices I make.

Permission Slip

I, your inner diva, give you full permission to step thoroughly into your values and allow those values to guide you in making healthy choices.

Double Diva Dare Ya!

To be mindful of the values that are most important to you this week and how they influence the choices you are making.

MVD

Most valuable diva

Power to the Kind Diva

The teen diva knows that when she practices kindness,
she becomes a pillar of peace in the world.

—Diva

You might be wondering how kindness could possibly be a power tool in today's world with so much, anger, violence, bullying, peer pressure, meanness, and competition out there. With so much negativity, it's natural to feel fear, anxiety, sadness, and anger. You might even think that you have to go on the defensive and join in with judgment and anger, perhaps even strike first, so you are not stricken. What a shame that those feelings have become so commonplace. I want you to understand something, my dear. By joining in the negativity and anger, you are adding to the problem rather than becoming part of the solution. Problems cannot be solved with the same energy that created them. Let me repeat that because this is so important to your success in life. *Problems cannot be solved with the same energy that created them.* Anger and hate breed more anger and hate and keeps conflicts going. The teen diva knows that being kind is not a weakness; being kind is strength. She knows that when she is kind, she becomes a pillar of peace in the world and a part of the solution. She is setting a new trend to make the world a better place—the place it was always intended to be.

Kindness can feel confusing and challenging at times. I mean, why show someone kindness who shows such contempt and anger, right? Wrong! Being kind doesn't mean that you excuse people for their negative behavior; that would mean you are enabling them to continue to behave negatively. Being kind simply means you appreciate that they have a story that brought them to where they are right now, attitudes and all, and you do it without judgment. You have no idea what they are enduring in other areas of their life that makes them act the way they do. Being kind means reaching out to offer some support, a little outside perspective, and encouragement. A simple act of kindness can change not only one person's world but yours as well. When you exercise compassion by recognizing that there is a story you know nothing about, and that has nothing to do with you, kindness won't be so difficult.

At the end of the day, you have to be happy with who you are and with the impact you've made in your life and the lives of those you encountered. Your simple acts of kindness will come back to you tenfold. You will get back what you give.

Use these ways to practice kindness:
- ◊ Leave a random note on someone's locker telling him or her you care.
- ◊ Share your lunch.
- ◊ Buy someone a cup of coffee.
- ◊ Put a positive message on someone's social media page.
- ◊ Pay a compliment.
- ◊ Offer to lend a helping hand.
- ◊ Stand up for someone.

Journal It!

- *What do you do on a regular basis to practice random acts of kindness?*
- *What inspires you to do those things?*
- *In what areas of your life do you need to better practice kindness? Why?*
- *What makes those areas a struggle for you?*
- *What can you do to stretch yourself to be more kind?*
- *If you are struggling to be kind in a certain area of your life, it's usually because someone or something is influencing your attitude. Who or what is influencing your unkind behavior? What does that say about you? What do you want people to say and feel about you? What would a diva do to be more kind?*

Mantra

Being a pillar of peace in the world is nothing more than a choice to be kind—always.

Permission Slip

I, your inner diva, give you full permission to become an example of how truly powerful kindness can be and start a new trend.

Double Diva Dare Ya!

To let go of taking on other people's attitudes. Instead, show up in a way that is so contagiously kind that they can't help but take on yours. Remember, people we don't think deserve to be treated kindly are often the ones who need to be shown kindness the most. They have a story; something made them that way. Be a diva and show them by your example that happiness and kindness are better choices and not far out of reach.

DPOP:

Diva pillar of peace

The Power of Thought and Intention

*The intention and emotion behind your thoughts
commits you to the outcome.*

—Diva

D iva girl, you are so smart, and I know you totally get how powerful your thoughts are. They are "diva-magically" powerful. They are the hocus-pocus of how your day begins, progresses, and eventually ends. They are magical because your thoughts determine how you feel, and how you feel determines how you act or, in some cases, don't act. For example, if you tell yourself you won't pass your math test because your teacher doesn't like you, you probably won't try as hard because you may feel hopeless. You may find yourself saying something like "Why bother? My teacher hates me, so why waste my time trying?" This observation sets your intention for the end result because you think that any effort will be a waste of time. The intention you have behind your thoughts commits you to creating the outcome of whatever it is you want or don't want.

Now, we all have days when we feel hopeless, frustrated, and simply can't see the light at the end of the tunnel—days when we don't feel like we are enough or have enough energy to give to accomplishing goals. Setting positive intentions can seem near impossible when past experiences dictate what you are feeling and thinking right now. However, staying stuck in that mind-set just keeps that reality, well, real. When you are struggling to set positive intentions, the trick is to challenge your experiences in a way that empowers you. Really consider what makes that thought true for you. Consider the lessons you learned from those experiences and how you can apply them going forward. Then set a new intention for a successful outcome, and believe it!

Journal It!

- *What is it that I want today?*
- *Why do I want it?*
- *How do I want to feel at the end of the day when I get it?*
- *What are some choices I can make today to make my desire a reality?*

Set an Intention

Using the template below, consider what you want to accomplish today and how you want to feel at the end of the day as a result. You've so got this!

I intend to _____ and feel *so* diva and _____ at the end of the day/week/month/year because I am a DITCH and _____.

Dantra

I am going to take back my power from past negative experiences and give that power to my thoughts and positive intentions, fully believing in my ability to create the outcome I desire.

Permission Slip

I, your inner diva, give you full permission to set positive intentions to create success every day. You are so diva and so worthy of the outcomes you wish!

Double Diva Dare Ya!

To pick one thing that wasn't successful in the past and that you believe will not change in the future. Now, change that belief to one that will work for you rather than against you. For example, "It might not have worked before, but with all that I learned from that experience, I've so got this now!" Feel the energy behind it, and let that energy drive your intentions to succeed. That's so diva!

The Power of Self-Control

No drama can be solved with the same dramatic attitude that created it.

—Diva

Sweet diva, one of the things that make girls so special and celebrated is the gift of sensitivity—our ability to truly feel our emotions. Emotions keep us connected to what's going on with us and around us. Our emotions drive us every single day. They drive our successes and our failures. They drive how much energy we have to complete a task and how we interact with others. Some days we may feel inspired and excited, which makes us productive and a joy to be around. Other days, hormones, a bad grade, or drama with friends and family may take us hostage and spin us out of control, causing us to feel rage, depression, anger, frustration, and sadness at the drop of a pin. When you factor in all that you have on your plate as a teenager, the pressures you are experiencing, and the changes you are going through, you probably feel like you are on an emotional roller-coaster ride on a regular basis. That's perfectly normal!

Sweetheart, emotions are very real. There are no silly emotions unless you are feeling, well, truly silly. And believe it or not, every emotion is a gift. Even emotions like anger and sadness are gifts because they are messengers telling us that something needs to change and a problem needs to be solved. The more positive emotions, such as happiness, joy, and peace, validate that we are on the right path. Another huge gift from our emotions is that they help us relate to others by building empathy and compassion. If we don't experience emotions, how can we possibly relate to and be compassionate and supportive with each other? The trick is in learning how to manage your emotions so they work for you rather than against you because if they are not managed well, they can fuel your problems rather than solve them. Remember, problems can't be solved with the same energy that created them.

Desdemona loves to stir up emotions in girls, and she loves to invite her best friend, GAIL, to join her in an effort to keep you stuck in negativity. What she doesn't realize is that you can use GAIL to get your emotions under control by better understanding her. Pssst, that's our secret though.

G—gremlins

A—assumptions

I—interpretations

L—limiting beliefs

Gremlins are like little trolls inside your brain put there by Desdemona. They make up the voice inside your head that lies to you and tells you that you are not good enough in some way.

◊ How do you think gremlins impact how well you control your emotions?

◊ What other power tools would you use to counter Desdemona and her gremlins so you can regain emotional control?

◊ What power phrase might be helpful in addressing gremlins?

Assumptions can really goof up a relationship and create unnecessary drama. Assumptions create a story that hasn't been written. They try to tell us that because something happened once before, it will *always* happen. For example, "My teacher didn't have time for me last week, so he'll *never* have time to help me get my grade up." Assumptions create unnecessary drama.

◊ How do you think assumptions impact your emotions?

◊ How can you challenge your assumptions so you can minimalize the amount of drama in your life?

◊ Are the assumptions you are making really true?

Interpretations also create a story. They throw in a little color and drama, and can leave you feeling like a victim. With interpretations, what someone says isn't always what the other person might hear. For example, your friend might comment on your new haircut and say something like "Wow! You got a lot cut off!" You might interpret that to mean, "Great, she thinks it's ugly."

◊ How do you think interpretations impact your emotions?

◊ What can you do to lessen the drama that interpretations might cause you and regain emotional control?

Limiting beliefs is like following the crowd and going with whatever the crowd says. For example, "Friendships are supposed to be full of drama, and that's just the way it is." Ick! That is definitely a drama creator, as it doesn't allow for optimism or hope. Healthy friendships are *not* full of drama. But when you have that belief, your thought about that belief creates your reality, and you will settle into the drama as if it is something you must endure.

◊   How do you think limiting beliefs impact your emotions?

◊   What can you do to challenge your limiting beliefs and create a more positive reality?

When you become aware of Desdemona and her friend GAIL, you have one of the greatest tools in your tool chest to manage your emotions and make better choices on how you respond to difficult situations and conflicts. The trick is to change your thoughts and beliefs in an empowering way—a way that seeks an opportunity to better understand yourself, others, and the situation in front of you. The secret is to be inquisitive with yourself and others to get clarity so you can better manage your emotions.

Journal It!

Think of situations where you experience a lot of conflict.
Now challenge GAIL by asking these questions:

- *What assumptions am I making that keep this conflict going?*
- *Am I creating a story that doesn't really exist?*
- *What am I reading into the conflict that might need clarity?*

- *Am I interpreting something the wrong way? Why?*
- *What can I do to get clarity and reach a resolution?*
- *What questions are burning in my heart that will help me gain clarity?*
- *What's really going on?*

Mantra

I have the tools to manage my emotions and feel in total control of myself and my outcomes.

Permission Slip

I, your inner diva, give you full permission to let go of any stories and misunderstandings that create drama in your life and instead gain total self-control by being super inquisitive and seeking clarity.

Double Diva Dare Ya!

To speak up and seek clarity when your emotions get stirred up. Most likely there is a big misunderstanding.

A Grateful Heart's Power

*An attitude of gratitude breaks the chains that have bound you
in negativity and gives you wings to fly freely on your journey,
seeing and believing in all that is good and possible.*

—Diva

racticing an attitude of gratitude allows you to see the true gift in every experience and keeps you positive and energized. Believe me, there is power in positivity! Positivity is powerful because it keeps you connected and focused on what is important to you, and it helps you attract the things you want in life. Practicing an attitude of gratitude also helps you shift your energy from a place of feeling like a victim of life to attaching more positive meaning to your experiences so you can stay happy and productive. There is *big* power in positivity!

There are lots of obvious joyful experiences that happen every day, such as receiving a surprise from a friend, getting a good grade on a test, taking a fun vacation, seeing a good movie, reading a good book, and having a great conversation. I could go on and on, but I think you get the idea. There are also experiences that might take a little more effort in which to find the gift, such as an argument with a friend or family member, a bad grade on a test, or a loss of some kind. Even in those experiences, you will learn something about yourself or be reminded of something that is important to you. Perhaps you can be grateful for the lesson and discovering even more deeply what you do or don't want in life. Perhaps you might learn something new about someone, and it strengthened your relationship. Perhaps you saw something that you might not otherwise have seen if you hadn't had your experience. That's huge!

Here are some ways to express and exercise gratitude:
- ◊ Keep a gratitude journal. At the end of the day, write all of the best things that happened.
- ◊ Be mindful of all the little things your day presented to you, such as a smile from a friend or a random compliment.
- ◊ Write a thank-you note to someone.
- ◊ Have a conversation with your inner diva and thank her for reminding you of how you do or don't want to be, and for the power she gives you to change and be the person you do want to be.
- ◊ Show your gratitude by giving someone a big hug and reminding that person of how special he or she is to you.
- ◊ Give all of your experiences meaning that works for you rather than against you. For example, for every unfortunate thing that happened to you today, follow it with "but fortunately ..." and list one good thing that came from it. Perhaps you dropped your books all over the hallway at school, but fortunately, someone nice helped you pick them up, and you made a new friend.

Dantra

Life and all experiences in life are a gift. I will find the gift and exercise an attitude of gratitude every day.

Permission Slip

I, your inner diva, give you full permission to look for the gift in every experience. If you find yourself crying, know that there is a gift in your tears too, for they are reminders of the things that are important to us. They also remind us of the blessings in our lives.

Double Diva Dare Ya!

To let go of the negative meanings you attach to your experiences and practice an attitude of gratitude instead. Look for the gift in every experience.

The Power of Language

Your word is your wand! That's so diva!

—Diva

Diva darling, your word is *so* magical. It's magic because it has the power to impact every minute of your day, your relationships, how you feel about yourself, people feel about you, and you make other people feel. What you say and the energy you put behind what you say has the power to make or break your day and someone else's day too.

You see, the words you use in every situation link you to certain thoughts that impact how you feel and then impact how you act and respond to people and events. Your words can make you feel energized, motivated, and really good about yourself, or really bad, stuck, and confused with minimal energy.

There are a few words that are real downers for a diva, so we'll start with them. Then you can come up with your own set of words that might be holding you back and eliminate them from your language.

The first word that needs to be eliminated from your vocabulary is *just*. When you use the word *just*, you minimize yourself (and others!) and limit what is possible. That makes Desdemona *so* happy because she wants to keep you living small, and it makes me *so* mad because you are more than enough and deserve to live abundantly.

How many times have you said, "I just want ..."? What the Desdemona? You want more than that—I know you do! Or how many times have you said, "I'm just ..."? WTD? You are *so* much more than "just." You are everything and anything you want to be. The trick is to start committing to being more and wanting more by using empowered language. Instead of using the word *just*, try reframing your sentence in a way that empowers you and makes you feel limitless. Sometimes it might be a matter of dropping the word *just* from the sentence, and other times you might have to reframe the whole darn thing. These are some examples:

◊ I *just* want to pass this test!
  • I want to pass this test!
  • If you want to kick it up a notch and use some power of intention for extra success, you could say, "I am *so* going to pass this test! I've studied hard and can't wait to see the results of my efforts!"
◊ I'm *just* a cast member in the play.
  • I *am* a part of the cast, which is really important because of all the things we do to make the play fun and engaging.
◊ I *just* want to find a group of friends I can hang out with.
  • I want to find good friends.
  • I *am* going to sign up for activities that interest me and find people to hang out with who share my interests, core values, and whom I can spend my free time with.

The next word that we divas can't stand is *typically*. This is another limiting word. It says that this is the way you've always done something, and you are not open to change or improvement. Do you see how Desdemona loves this word too? *Typically* keeps you (and others!) small and living in a fear-based mentality. We know that change is important to our growth even though it can be uncomfortable and scary. If you are not open to change, you are not moving forward or open to future successes. You stay stuck, and that is even more uncomfortable and scary. The teenage years are hard enough. Who wants to stay stuck in that frustrating mentality? Not the diva! The best way to combat *typically* is to throw in a *but*. For example, "Typically we've done things this way, *but* let's think of some other ways we can kick things up a notch."

The last word I'm going to give you before you create your own list is *can't*. The word *can't* commits you to being uncommitted. It commits you to not even trying. It's an energy zapper, and what's worse is it sets you up for failure before you even try. It sets the intention that something won't work, and that sets the tone for your energy level, emotions, and how hard you will try. Replace the word *can't* with a word that is more empowering, such as *can, will,* or *commit*.

I want you to remember to walk your talk. While you are working on not minimizing yourself, be mindful not to minimize others. Always be kind.

Journal It!

- *What are your word habits?*
- *Are your word habits empowering you to live largely or keeping you stuck and small?*
- *How do your word habits contribute to how you feel about yourself?*
- *How are your words making other people feel about you?*
- *How are your words making other people feel about themselves?*
- *Make a list of some words that might hold you back or keep you stuck. Commit to eliminating them from your language.*
- *Now write a word that you can use to replace the negative word.*

Dantra

When I speak in a way that empowers me, it also empowers those around me. I choose to stand in my confidence and speak in a way that makes me feel energized and good, as well as make others feel good. Nothing is impossible because I'm possible!

Permission Slip

I, your inner diva, give you full permission to use your words as your wand and create magic in your life and the lives of others.

Double Diva Dare Ya!

To let go of negative language that keeps you stuck and living small. You are so much more than "just," and believe me, diva girl, you can do anything and be anything.

WTD?

What the Desdemona?

MWIMW:

My word is my wand

The Teen Diva's Bill of Rights*

The teen diva has the right
- ◊ to respect herself and be treated with respect in return—fearlessly;
- ◊ to practice happiness and be genuinely happy;
- ◊ to make empowered choices;
- ◊ to love and be loved;
- ◊ to step fully into who she is in every beautiful way;
- ◊ to be free from bullying, judgment, and ridicule;
- ◊ to stand up for what is right;
- ◊ to be free from discrimination in any way;
- ◊ to be balanced;
- ◊ to belong and be a part of something meaningful;
- ◊ to have healthy and positive friendships and relationships;
- ◊ to live by her morals and values;
- ◊ to dream and make those dreams become reality;
- ◊ to fearlessly and beautifully define herself;
- ◊ to be healthy in mind, body, and spirit;
- ◊ to be free from ignorance;
- ◊ to be free from insecurities;
- ◊ to be heard and a part of solutions;
- ◊ to inspire;
- ◊ to make mistakes;
- ◊ to be fully seen for her divaness;
- ◊ to celebrate being a girl;

◊ to be accountable;

◊ to set boundaries;

◊ to stand for love, life, humanity, and respect;

◊ to celebrate who she is—her character, her values, her beliefs, her spirit, her body, her mind, her radiance, her tenderness, her magical presence, her courage, her brilliance, and every ounce of her being; and

◊ **to live—fearlessly!**

*The Teen Diva's Bill of Rights requires all who exercise these rights also to respect them with others.

Chapter 2

Identity for the Teen Diva

The Teen Diva's Identity Crisis

When you understand what makes you love greatly, laugh contagiously, cry intensely, anger passionately, and be blissfully happy, you will more deeply understand who you are.

—Diva

"Who am I?" the teen diva asks herself. "Where do I fit in?" Welcome to your teenage years. These are two of the most difficult questions for a teen diva to answer. The good news is that you are on a journey to discovering the answers. The bad news is that my evil sister, Desdemona, will try to confuse you by defining who you are, where you fit, and what to do to fit in. She might even recruit others to influence you, such as the media, people in your communities, bullies, and society in general. If you stick with me, I will be your armor against Desdemona and give you the positive tools you need to define yourself so *you* can choose who you are, who you will become, where you fit, and how to fit.

The teenage years for a diva are some of the most wonderful and yet the most challenging. You're not quite an adult yet, but you're not a child anymore either. You are in that in-between space. You are starting off in newer and bigger schools, which means you will be choosing and making new friends, and your classes will be getting more difficult. You will be trying to keep up with school, what's cool, fashion, and friends, and you will be starting to explore relationships. Your body is going through changes, which means your emotions are changing too. At times, you may feel completely out of control, but trust me ... it will be okay! I mean, who wouldn't feel out of control with all of *that* on their plates? Eeks!

Finding out who you are is a journey, and this is the beginning. The answer will evolve as you grow because all things change with time. Five years from now, you will not be the same person you are right now. Your priorities will change. Your responsibilities will change. Your interests will change. Your boundaries will change. And your character will continue to evolve and grow. You will constantly be learning about the most important character and subject in your life: you!

Many people attach labels to describe who they are, such as daughter, friend, sister, student, athlete, or dancer, and tall, short, thin, heavy, blond, or brunette. Those are roles that you play, which are a part of who you are but not *really* who you are. And your physical appearance is nothing more than a shell that carries and protects who you truly are and the truest part of yourself—your heart, your values, your personality, your passions, your character, and everything that makes you come alive.

Who you are is so much more than the roles you play in your life or your appearance. Who you are has everything to do with what is centered in your heart—the things that make you come alive, the things that ignite a bright and beautiful flame within you.

I want you to remember something essential: The Desdemonas of the world will try to blow out your flame by negatively defining you, pointing out your weaknesses, and telling you every reason why you are limited. They might even try to alter your values and character by convincing you to go against some of what's important to you if you want to be cool and fit in. What they are really trying to do is throw you off track from a cool and bright future. Remember, *cool* is a subjective word and means something different to everyone. Nobody can define what *cool* is but *you*. And that is pretty cool!

The divas of the world will remind you of everything wonderful about you, your gifts, your strengths, and your amazing character; that's what is most important. They will pick you up when you fall, dust you off, and remind you that you are stronger and more beautiful because of it. They will let you know that the fall is part of your story and doesn't define you. They will remind you of your grace, beauty, gifts, and strengths, so you can write your story differently going forward. The divas in the world will not allow you to feel hopeless or less than perfect because they know that with you in this world, there is great hope for the world.

Desdemona and her army might try to blow out your flame, but with me around, your flame cannot be extinguished. Keep shining on, diva! Keep shining on!

Journal It!
Who are you right now?
Everyone has an inner diva, a goddess. Give your goddess a name of your own. What are your greatest gifts? How do you share those gifts with the world? What are your values? How do those values show up in your character and the way you interact with others? How do you make people around you feel? What are your interests and passions? What lights you up?

Who do others think you are?

What do others say about you? Would they say you are smart, driven, funny, athletic, kind? Do they limit you with their beliefs? Do you agree with them? Why? What can you do right now to take back your power from their definition and fully own your positive definition of who you are?

Where do you fit?

If you have a size eight foot but the shoes you want to buy only have a size seven left, would you buy that pair of shoes, squeeze into them, and live uncomfortably? I would hope not! They would give you blisters and cause you pain and anguish. Your feet might look stylish in your new shoes, but you will be walking around panting and groaning with every step. This idea applies to you socially too. Do you fit where it feels good and comfortable? Do you fit where your passions and interests are? Do you fit with those who match your values and keep you safe?

Dantra

Who I am and who I will become is entirely about me staying true to my values and my ever-loving divamazing character! I fully own who I am and who I want to become. My inner goddess and I can do and manifest anything we put our hearts to.

Double Diva Dare Ya!

To write your name and your goddess name on a piece of paper, and then write a definition of yourself using your greatest gifts and how you let your gifts shine every day. Keep it where you can see it, and affirm it by saying, "I am so diva!"

75

Power Tools: Which tools would you use and how would you use them?

- *Assertiveness*
- *Bill of rights*
- *Boundaries*
- *Character*
- *Choices*
- *Compassion*
- *Confidence*
- *Gratitude*
- *Kindness*
- *Language*
- *Ownership*
- *Power phrase*
- *Self-control*
- *Thought and intention*
- *Values*
- *Your voice*

*What else will be helpful?*_____

IASD!:
I am so diva!

MAMIG:
Me and my inner goddess

How The Teen Diva Defines Herself

The way in which you judge and define others says a lot about who you are and how you judge and define yourself. Always be kind to yourself and others.

—Diva

Why is it that it's easier to remember the bad stuff people say to us or about us than the good stuff? Why is it that we accept the negativity and judgments from others as being the truth? Worse yet, why do we take those judgments and definitions, own them, and validate the bullies in our lives by living according to their judgments as the truth? That's no way to live, sweet diva! Remember, the way people treat you says a lot about who they really are and how they feel about themselves. If they are criticizing you, they have "stuff" that they want to get rid of so they try to put their stuff in your "all." It doesn't belong there! Don't judge them for their critical ways, or you are no better than they are and would be breeding the same negative energy.

The way in which you judge and define others says a lot about who you are and how you define yourself. In some ways, it serves as a reminder of what's really important to you: your values. On the other hand, judging reveals negative traits like ignorance since we are not built from a "one size fits all" model. We each have had unique experiences that have made us who we are in this moment. As you begin this journey of self-discovery, it's important to remember that what's important, meaningful, and purposeful to one person may not have the same importance and meaning to you. Remember, always be kind to yourself and to others, being mindful that you are special and unique, and have a brand of beauty and gifts that are only yours to own.

So what really defines who you are? Defining who you are means that you pick out the best parts of yourself—your characteristics, values, passions, interests, and features—that make you come alive. You take these parts and own them. I mean you *really* own them and wear them like a diva badge of honor, holding on to them so tightly that there is no way the Desdemonas of the world can possibly take them away from you. Defining yourself is about reaching deep inside and embracing all of the things that make you curious, charismatic, special, and unique, *without* the influence of others.

Let's take a trip back in time. As a small child, you had natural interests, and gravitated toward certain activities. Perhaps you loved tumbling, dancing, or gymnastics. Perhaps you enjoyed sports. Perhaps you enjoyed playing dress-up, putting on makeup, playing house, or pretending to be a princess. Maybe you had a chemistry kit and loved science. Or maybe you liked to bake. Your younger years were full of creativity, curiosity, and exploration. You were able to see the beauty and wonder in so much! Your curiosities and creativity were limitless, and you sought out the things that brought you happiness. You were most genuinely you! It's unlikely that anyone influenced whether or not those things were cool; you followed your bliss in the moment.

So what changes in the teenage years? Why do these years seem to be so difficult and confusing? Why doesn't bliss come as easily anymore? Why is it so easy to get lost during these years? As a teenager, you are likely going to larger schools, your curiosities are changing, your relationships are changing, and there are pressures and influences all around you to meet the definitions of what society, the media, and your peers believe to be a beautiful and successful teenage girl. This can feel overwhelming and naturally leave you confused. In the midst of the changes you are experiencing, you might find yourself seeking answers and approval from the outside, or allowing yourself to be "under the influence" of others telling you who you are, who to be, what's cool, what's not cool, and what beauty and success look like.

As you move forward on your journey, it's important to remember that what's cool, beauty, success, and purpose are all subjective—they mean something different to everyone. For example, success to one person might mean studying hard and making the dean's list, getting into an Ivy League college, climbing the corporate ladder, and making millions of dollars. Success to another might be joining the Peace Corps to make a difference in the lives of people who are struggling in third world countries. Beauty to one girl might mean wearing designer clothes and makeup and staying in line with the latest fashion trends. Beauty to another might mean living naturally and having a vibrant and unique personality. True beauty and success to a diva can only be defined by her own eyes and is all about remaining true to who she is and to her passions, her interests, and her values.

Beauty and success are unique to every individual, but many find it incomprehensible that being different is a good thing and strive to be just like everyone else. When you strive to look and act just like everyone around you, you will most likely get lost and stuck because you no longer stand out from the crowd—nothing makes you unique anymore. You might even wind up walking in the shadows of others who are influencing your path. You will know that you are going against who you are because you will feel a sense of suffering and unhappiness and a lack of bliss.

So, how *do* you define yourself at a time in your life when there are so many outsiders influencing and labeling you? How do you know that you are being true to yourself? Your emotions will be your messengers. They will remind you of what's really important and who you really are. Listen.

1. When the teen diva knows she is being true to herself and living by her most authentic definition, she will feel bliss, confidence, and happiness. This is when the teen diva is fully honoring and embracing her inner diva.

2. When the teen diva is not being true to herself and is living instead by the definitions of outside influence, she will feel discomfort, distraction, and a lack of joy. At this point, she has the power to choose differently and honor what makes her feel blissful again.

My sweet teen diva, I give you full permission to love yourself for who you are right now, who you choose to be, where you choose to go, and what you choose to do. I give you permission to define yourself in a way that will help you to achieve every dream—to truly embrace who you are in every way and let that light shine and guide you. You are beautiful. You are successful. You are naturally captivating. You are unique. You have purpose. You have style. Follow your bliss and stay true to yourself.

Journal It!

As you begin your journey of self-discovery, be super inquisitive and ask why on a regular basis. "Why?" will keep you attached to what's most important to you (your values) and keep you strong. When you are living in line with your values, you are living in line with your truest self: your diva.

These are some good questions to consider:

- *Why do I want this?*
- *Why do I want to explore this?*
- *Why do I like this style?*
- *Why is this important to me?*
- *Why do I want to be friends with a particular group?*
- *Why do I want to pursue _____?*
- *Why do I keep _____ when it makes me feel _____?*
- *Why do I get so upset when _____?*

Dantra

Beauty and success are subjective; they mean something different to everyone. I choose to stay true to myself and own my unique definition of what beauty and success are for me. I choose to stand in and live my own truth. I do not need and will not choose to seek the approval of others to step into and fully own my uniquely captivating, beautiful, and purposeful self.

Let it Go!

Let go of standing in the shadows of others, of trying to be just like everyone else and not fully seen. You were born unique and to stand out shining with purpose. It's the world's privilege to see your light shine, and it's your honor and duty to share it with the world.

Double Diva Dare Ya!

To write a list of everything that makes you uniquely gifted and beautiful—what makes you shine! If you are in a place of struggle, talk to your best friend to get you started. Then I challenge you to take at least one thing on your list and consciously use that unique and beautiful piece of yourself fearlessly every day in your conversations, activities, and so on.

Power Tools: Which tools would you use and how would you use them?

- *Boundaries*
- *Character*
- *Choices*
- *Compassion*
- *Confidence*
- *Language*
- *Power phrase*
- *Values*

What else will be helpful? _____

FLMDT:

Fearlessly living my diva truth

DBOH:

Diva badge of honor

Divas Think Outside of the Box

True freedom for the teen diva begins when she steps outside of the box that has confined her and into unlimited creative space to define her unique style, brand of beauty, and success.

—Diva

hat does it mean to "think outside of the box"? Perhaps we should talk about what it means to be boxed in first. Boxed-in thinking means you are closed off to new possibilities. It means you are choosing to stand still and do things as they have always been done. Boxed-in thinking keeps you stuck in mediocrity and can make you feel like a victim of life, never seeing possibilities, solving problems, or growing into the amazing young woman that you truly are and meant to become. Boxed-in thinking is the work of Desdemona. After all, her goal is to rob you of creating, expressing, and stepping fully into who you are. And, of course, she's out to keep you living and being small.

I want you to consider for a minute all of the ways you are boxing yourself in with your thinking and who or what is influencing you and keeping you boxed in and living small. How much are you living by someone else's image of who you are? Are friends influencing you to be or act a certain way? Is social media influencing you to look or act a certain way? Are models and the media's measuring stick influencing you about what a beautiful and successful teenage girl should be? Do you feel like none of this fits? Of course it doesn't fit! There isn't a one-size-fits-all model in life. Your life is a gift, and you have your own unique gifts and purpose to share with the world. You have your own unique brand of beauty and can define your own success. You get to create, embrace, and *be* your own unique diva with your unique diva charm. But you must step outside of the box and change your way of thinking, leaving all that is not serving you and feeding your life inside the box. Then kick that box to the curb, and don't look back!

Boxed-in thinking is nothing more than a habit that easily can be changed. (Big *but* alert!) *But* ... before that habit can be changed, you have to acknowledge and change your thought processes about who you are right now and be willing to imagine, dream, and take action to become who you want to be. You have to imagine that anything is possible in life. You have to go beyond *typically* and move into *possibility*.

Thinking outside of the box is really important. Life, and all of the pressures that go along with it, is hard enough. When you practice outside-of-the-box thinking, you are on the road to reducing insanity and stress. It stops you at the edge of mediocrity and catapults you into greatness, creativity, and all that is possible. There are *so* many diva benefits to outside-of-the-box thinking:

◊   It exercises leadership skills.

◊   It exercises creativity.

◊   It keeps you positive and seeing possibilities. You will be less likely to get stuck in a victim mentality.

◊   It solves problems.

◊   It helps you discover, define, and own who you are.

◊   It helps you break the chains of influence.

It might feel kind of scary when you start exercising outside-of-the-box thinking. I mean, it's new and different from what you have been used to. It has been comfortable doing things as they have always been done. But by doing things as they have always been done, nothing changes and you stay living in mediocrity.

Follow these tips for living outside of the box:

◊   Remember, what is inside the box is confining. Your space and choices are limited (if you even have choices inside the box).

◊   Remember, what is outside of the box is limitless space and creativity. The possibilities are endless.

◊   Put yourself in an environment that inspires you and influences you positively—an environment that allows you to daydream and come up with outside-of-the-box ideas.

◊   Surround yourself with others who live outside of the box—people who encourage you to be your best, to dream and work toward making those dreams a reality.

◊ Remove these words from your language immediately:
  • Typically
  • Should
  • Just
  • Have to
  • Need to
  • Can't
  • Won't
  • Impossible (replace with I'm possible.)

◊ Think about whatever you are trying to solve at the moment. Now think about the lesson (the gift!) the problem is trying to teach you. Then, remaining totally positive and optimistic, consider every possibility. Exercise your own unique creativity here.

◊ Remember, you don't have to do it alone. Asking other divas, parents, teachers, and mentors for support is totally okay.

◊ Remember, together we are better and stronger. Together we are magical!

Journal It!

- *Imagine yourself thinking freely and breaking the chains that have kept you bound inside of the box. What does it feel like to be so free?*
- *Write about all possibilities that move you and get you excited. Do some visioning work. Brainstorm.*
- *Consider creating a vision board that shows who you want to become and what you want to accomplish. This is a great thing to do because it keeps your vision in front of you.*

Dantra

I choose to step outside of the box and into total creative freedom, living in an unlimited space of possibilities and success.

Let it Go!

Kick that box and all of the negativity confined within it to the curb. It isn't serving your highest good, your diva.

Double Diva Dare Ya!

To find a problem within your community and create an outside-of-the-box plan to solve the problem. You don't have to actually solve the problem if you don't want to, but at least create a plan so you can exercise possibilities and your leadership skills.

Power Tools: Which tools would you use and how would you use them?

- *Assertiveness*
- *Boundaries*
- *Choices*
- *Confidence*
- *Language*
- *Ownership*
- *Power phrase*
- *Thought and intention*
- *Values*
- *Your voice*

What else will be helpful? _____

Your Captivation Factor

When you are captivating, it is clear to the world that
you are living fully in your bliss.

—Diva

OMD! *Captivation* is quite a word! And once again it's a word that means something different to everyone because we are unique and have different values, characters, and ideas of what is captivating. What one person finds captivating, another person might find boring, mundane, or, well, you decide what adjective you want to use. Our differences and ability to see beauty in things that others might not is part of what makes this world so interesting and magnificent. It's also what causes unfair judgments.

There is a reason I am making that point. To remind you that judgment has nothing to do with you and everything to do with the person who's acting all judgmental. It's that person's story, perception, and differences from you that are causing him or her to judge. Don't take that individual's stuff and put it in your all. It's not really about you, and it doesn't have any meaning about you until you give it meaning.

There's no need to inflict unnecessary drama on yourself by doing that, right? Of course, we all want to be captivating and impressive to everyone, but that would be unreal because it would mean that we are all the same. How boring! Not captivating at all. So *not* diva.

So what does it mean to be captivating? First, captivating is something you already are; you need to set it free for others to see. It requires a dose of courage and a little bit of work. To be captivating requires enthusiasm for your passions, experiences, successes, and interests. When you are truly captivating, it is clear to the world that you are living in your bliss. When you are captivating, there is mysteriousness about you, and people naturally want to learn more. To be truly captivating requires you to step fully into your bliss by breaking any spell of fear or doubt that Desdemona may have cast on you and choosing instead to live happily, fearlessly, and *you*niquely.

Try these tips to show the world how captivating you are:
◊ Speak passionately and positively
◊ Be optimistic
◊ Share your wisdom and knowledge
◊ Show that you are open minded to hearing many perspectives and offer up your varying perspectives
◊ Be solutions minded
◊ Be yourself!
◊ Radiate love in the way you speak, act, and for the things you are passionate about

Journal It!

- *What are you doing when you are in your bliss?*
- *Where have those experiences taken you?*
- *What do those experiences teach you about yourself?*
- *Where do you want those experiences to take you?*
- *In what ways do you share those experiences?*
- *What do you need to let go of, or what spell of Desdemona's do you need to break in order to become more captivating?*

Dantra

I am uniquely captivating.

Let it Go!

Let go of all negativity, self-loathing, and self-doubt that holds you back from your captivation factor.

Double Diva Dare Ya!

To step outside of your comfort zone this week and try something new that will add to your captivation factor.

Power Tools: Which tools would you use and how would you use them?

- *Character*
- *Confidence*
- *Language*
- *Ownership*
- *Power phrase*
- *Values*
- *Your voice*

What else will be helpful? _____

BYADC:

Be youniquely and divaly captivating

Make Happiness a Priority

True happiness is the freedom to be be-you-tifully
and fearlessly yourself.

—Diva

To be able to positively define yourself, you have to know what keeps you positive and deeply understand all that makes you happy. Until you wrap your mind around this information, it's understandable that happiness can sometimes seem far out of reach. I want you to know that you can experience happiness right now!

There are tons of reasons why happiness can be a struggle. Some teens (actually one in four) are bullied. Some are in tough situations at home. Some are struggling to get good grades. Some are completely overwhelmed with everything on their plate and struggle to find balance. Some don't feel like they measure up to what they're told a successful and beautiful teenage girl should be, and they are constantly competing with the media's measuring stick and their peers' influences. You get the point: happiness can be a struggle. However, it *is* accessible to you right now. In fact, the "now moment" is the only place where joy can be experienced. It's impossible to change your past experiences to happy ones, and future experiences are yet to be created. Happiness can only be experienced now.

To define yourself in a way that will help you experience more happiness in your life, you have to know what happiness means to you—what it looks like, what it feels like, and *how* you are going to experience it. You also need to know what despair and unhappiness look like so you are clear about what robs you of your joy because Desdemona is quite the joy thief. By knowing what robs you of your joy, you can armor yourself with some of your power tools to counter Desdemona or anyone else who tries to bring you down. Knowing what makes you happy (and unhappy) is important stuff. You need this information to make conscious choices and to create and own your identity. You need this information to experience happiness on your journey, knowing it is accessible to you right now. When you know what causes your suffering and unhappiness, you have great power to choose differently and experience more genuine happiness—more diva bliss.

Shawn Achor, the author of *The Happiness Advantage* and a professor at Yale University, says people don't become happy when they find success, but that happiness will actually determine your success. Happier people tend to attract greater success in life. So if you choose to engage in activities and surround yourself with people who keep you positive, your chance for success is greater. That can be difficult as a teenager because there is so much drama and external influence. As a teen, it's easy to get lost in what everyone else thinks. That's the first thing you need to let go of—being influenced by what others think. Choosing happiness means not worrying if what you are doing is in alignment with someone else's definition of happiness or what others say is cool. Remember, *cool* is subjective and means something different to everyone. Well, happiness is subjective too! One person might find happiness doing things that wouldn't fit the mold for another person's happiness. Happiness is choosing to do things that create good feelings within *you*. It means staying true to your values, beliefs, character, and passions, and keeping your eye on your goals while enjoying the journey to reach your goals. It's also what makes you captivating!

You have a choice to make. You can choose to put yourself in situations that bring you down and leave you feeling bitter and lost, or you can choose to put yourself in situations and surround yourself with people that feed your beautiful spirit, keep you true to yourself, and fill your days with what makes you happy. The most important decision you can make right now is to choose to experience happiness now. Immerse yourself in the things that make you blissfully happy—things that are aligned with the truest parts of yourself, your interests, and your passions—and bliss will continue to be yours.

Journal It!

- *What does happiness look like to you?*
- *Describe your ideal day and the things that make you happy.*
- *Who and what influence your happiness? If you are not happy, who or what is influencing your lack of happiness?*
- *What is a lack of happiness in your life costing you at home, at school, in your relationships?*
- *What would you gain if you created more happiness in your life?*

- *Who do you love spending time with? Who makes you laugh the hardest and makes you feel like you can do anything?*
- *Think of a time when you were really happy. What were you doing?*
- *How can you incorporate more of those things into your life to increase your happiness?*
- *How do you create your day in a way that inspires happiness?*
- *What can you do to create more happiness around you every day?*

Mantra

I choose to incorporate more happiness in my life and make it a priority. I choose to experience happiness now. I am worthy of every bit of happiness and success that life has to offer.

Let it Go!

Let go of negativity and living by what others say happiness is. Define happiness for yourself!

Double Diva Dare Ya!

To do something this week that brings more happiness into your life, fearlessly, without the influence of others.

Power Tools: Which tools would you use and how would you use them?

- *Assertiveness*
- *Bill of rights*
- *Boundaries*
- *Choices*
- *Gratitude*
- *Language*
- *Power phrase*
- *Thought and intention*
- *Values*
- *Your voice*

What else will be helpful? _____

2BHI2HMD:

To be happy is to honor my diva

MHAP:

Make happiness a priority

Plant the Seed, Not the Weed

When I choose to change how I present myself, those around me will change how they perceive me.

—Diva

o you ever feel like some people have crazy ideas about who you are and what you are capable or incapable of? You can't help but sit back and think, *O-M-D! Where did they get* that? Or *What the (bleeping!) Desdemona did I do to deserve* that? Without realizing it, you might be planting weeds in their minds and giving them information to feed their ideas about you by the way you present yourself. It might be the things you say, your body language, or your attitude. Often the information you give them is totally false because you are naturally awesome. You need to send a more accurate message to those around you by adjusting how you present yourself.

How many times do you make fun of yourself, criticize yourself, or cut yourself down in front of others? How many times do you stay quiet or feel afraid to be seen or heard for fear that you'll make a fool of yourself? These behaviors plant weeds in others' minds about you. This can spiral into some tough, unintended consequences, such as being picked last for the team because something you said may have sent an inaccurate message about your ability. Perhaps people will see you as being unapproachable or snobby when you are actually really sweet but quiet and a little bit shy. Some people might not ask for your help because at some point they might have been given the impression by you that you are not "enough" in some way. If you are okay with these results, fully own it and be happy. If you are unhappy with such results, fully own it and choose to send a different message. It's up to you!

If you are confused by the false assumptions or statements people make about you, I want you to think about how *you* present yourself to them. What weeds have you planted by saying or doing certain things? I want you to understand that when you choose to change the way you present yourself to the people around you, those people will change how they perceive you. When you refrain from speaking negatively about yourself and plant beautiful seeds in other people's minds, they will start to see the positive and beauty in you.

Diva Tips

◊ Focus on the things you are proud of, the things you like about yourself—your strengths—and proudly display them. Wear them like a DBOH!

◊ Change your statement to work *for* you rather than *against* you.

♦ Weed: I can't believe I did that. I'm so stupid.

♦ Seeds: I *am* a smart girl. I'm not sure what happened today, but I'm going to figure it out so next time I *will* totally succeed.

♦ Weed: I could never …

♦ Seeds: That looks hard, but I'm sure I can handle it.

Journal It!

- In what ways do I plant weeds in people's minds about who I am and my abilities?
- How do I really want people to see me?
- What seeds can I start planting today to show my real diva truth to those around me?

Dantra

I choose to present myself in a way that is empowering and plant positive seeds about me in the minds of others.

Let it Go!

Let go of self-loathing, self-shaming, and the insecurities that show the world what you are not because you are so much more!

Double Diva Dare Ya!

To be mindful of planting positive seeds about yourself in the statements and behaviors you display this week. Then let me know what changed!

Power Tools: Which tools would you use and how would you use them?

- *Character*
- *Choices*
- *Compassion*
- *Confidence*
- *Language*
- *Power phrase*
- *Your voice*

What else will be helpful? _____

PADS:

Planting a diva seed

Chapter 3

Managing Drama, Stress, and Balance

The Power of No

Every time you say yes to something that makes you uncomfortable, you are saying no to what is important and what really matters. Stay true to you!

—Diva

Yes! I mean I don't know, maybe. I mean let me think about it. *Ahhh!* No. For such a small word, it can sometimes be a big challenge to say. We girls tend to struggle with this word regardless of if it's in our best interest or not. Why? There could be a million reasons. Is it because we are afraid of letting someone else down? Is it because we fear missing out on something? Or is it because we fear not being liked, accepted, or cool? Are we trying to win someone's approval? *No* requires great courage to say and can also require courage to accept when it comes from others.

Every decision you make in life will require a yes or no answer, and that is scary stuff. Why is it scary? It's scary because it requires us to commit to and act on something. Every decision you make will affect you in some way, shaping who you will become in the future—whether it's tomorrow, next week, next year, or ten years from now. This can be challenging if you don't have the right tools to make those decisions.

The key to making "yes or no" decisions is to first say *yes* to respecting yourself physically, spiritually, academically, and emotionally. If you need time to think something through before committing, be assertive and ask for the time you need. Then begin with the end in mind. Close your eyes and picture what your decision will look like once it's made. What do you want the end result to be? What is the best possible outcome of the end result? What is the worst possible outcome? What might happen if you say yes? What might happen if you say no? How do you want to feel?

No is a powerful and courageous way for a diva to respect and protect herself, manage priorities, and define boundaries. No is a powerful way for a diva to acknowledge and respect her worth. If you are saying yes to things you are uncomfortable with, you are saying no to your morals and values—the things that make you the amazing teen diva you are. If you are uncomfortable with what is being asked of you, you will feel it in your gut and know that something isn't right. If something feels right, you will know that by the excitement and anticipation in your heart—that's me by the way, your inner diva!

Diva girl, you know that kindness is not a weakness; it's strength and a power tool. I want you to understand that saying no isn't mean or unkind. It stops you at the edge and protects you from taking a fall that might hurt. The way you approach the word *no* is what differentiates you (the teen diva!) from the Desdemonas in the world. Here are some ways to approach the word *no*:

◊ No, I can't commit to that right now but good luck!
◊ No, I'm already committed this weekend, but have fun and send me pics!
◊ Nope, I am not comfortable.

105

◊   No, it's not the right time for me, but I'll let you know if and when I'm ready.
◊   Something about this doesn't jive with me, but let me know how it goes.
◊   No, my health is really important to me.
◊   That's out of the question.
◊   Nah, totally not my thing.
◊   Thumbs down.
◊   No. There's really nothing you can say to make me change my mind.
◊   No. (It's a complete sentence.)
◊   Go fish.
◊   Ding! This diva's done!

Journal It!

- *List everything you want to say yes to in your life.*
- *List everything you want to say no to in your life.*
- *What are you saying yes to that is not in alignment with your goals, morals, and values—who you truly are?*
- *What can you do this week to start saying yes to what really matters and no to the things that block you from being, doing, and achieving?*

Dantra

When I say yes to things I am uncomfortable with, I am saying no to my morals and values. Today I start only saying yes and making decisions that are in my best interest and in line with what's really important to me. It's a courageous exercise in honoring my self-worth, and I am so worthy of all that is good for me!

Let it Go!

Let go of the belief that the more you say yes, the more you will be liked and respected. Don't allow yourself to become Debbie Doormat.

Double Diva Dare Ya!

To think of something you feel pressured to do that you don't feel comfortable with, something that goes against your values and morals. This is a sign that you are not honoring your inner diva. Courageously and fearlessly say no, knowing that you are standing on your self-worth.

Power Tools: Which tools would you use and how would you use them?

- *Assertiveness*
- *Bill of rights*
- *Boundaries*
- *Choices*
- *Compassion*
- *Confidence*
- *Language*
- *Ownership*
- *Values*
- *Your voice*

What else will be helpful? _____

NIACS:

No is a complete sentence

D!TDID!:

Ding! This diva is done!

It's Okay to Say It's Not Okay

"It's okay that you hurt me," said no diva ever!

—Diva

D ivas totally understand that mistakes happen, right? Sometimes those mistakes hurt us, and sometimes we make mistakes that might hurt someone else. There's nothing that can be done to turn back time and erase the hurt, but you can choose to make things right and apologize, and you can also choose to accept an apology.

Accepting an apology doesn't mean what someone did to you was okay. In fact, I don't ever recommend responding to an apology with "that's okay" because it's not okay, and in a weird way, you are giving someone permission to do it again by saying "that's okay." Accepting an apology is an act of compassion for you and the other person. By holding on to anger, hurt, and guilt, you are holding on to feelings of being victimized, and we know what that does, right? It zaps our energy, robs us of our personal power, and keeps us stuck. You don't deserve to be stuck, dear Diva! By letting go of the anger, hurt, and guilt with an apology and some forgiveness, you open up space within you that you need to keep moving forward. It's also an opportunity for you to set a boundary. If and when you choose to accept an apology, here are some empowered ways to do so:

◊ Thanks, I accept your apology.
◊ Mistakes happen. Thanks for acknowledging the mistake that was made.
◊ I was really hurt by what you did. Thanks for the apology.
◊ I think we both learned something from this experience. *State what you learned.* I appreciate you apologizing, and I'm sorry too.
◊ Thanks. I forgive you. I'd like to understand why you did what you did, and how I might have contributed.
◊ I appreciate your apology, and hope you will consider my feelings next time.
◊ Trust and loyalty are really important to me. Would you please do something to make things right for me?
◊ I really value our friendship and appreciate your thoughtfulness in apologizing.

What Would a Diva Do?

A diva would apologize and make things right if she hurt someone. She would also accept an apology without saying "it's okay" and set a boundary if needed. Not everyone comes forward to apologize. If someone hurts a diva and no apology is made, she can do a couple of things:

◊ She can choose to let it go by taking the lesson with her and choosing (for example) to spend time with people who match her values of loyalty and trust.

◊ She can choose to assert herself and start a conversation with the other person, expressing how the mistake made her feel. For example, "Hey, I want to clear the air on something. I'm really bummed out that _____. Help me understand what happened."

Journal It!

- *What do you keep saying, "it's okay" to?*
- *What is that costing you?*
- *In what ways can you address "it's okay" with the person who continues to cross the line with you?*
- *What boundaries do you need to set?*
- *What apologies do you need to make to someone else?*
- *How do you think a diva would handle boundaries and forgiveness?*

Dantra

It's okay to say it's not okay.

Let It Go!

Let go of the self-sabotaging attitude that makes you believe that "it's okay" when people have wronged you. Plant a new, more empowered seed that says something great about your self-worth.

Double Diva Dare Ya!

To forgive someone who has wronged you by either letting it go emotionally from your heart or addressing it with the individual and setting a boundary.

Power Tools: Which tools would you use and how would you use them?

- *Bill of rights*
- *Boundaries*
- *Character*
- *Choices*
- *Compassion*
- *Language*
- *Power phrase*
- *Your voice*

What else will be helpful? _____

IOKTSINOK:

It's okay to say it's not okay

The Drama Queen Dropout

If you have an excessive amount of drama in your life, you've probably created it in some way or have invited people into your life who so generously like to share it with you.

—Diva

iva darling, drama doesn't just walk into your life and follow you around. If you have drama in your life, you've probably created it in some way or have invited people into your life who like to share it with you. The teenage years can be full of drama if you allow it. There's the drama of added pressures and tighter schedules. There's the drama of taking tests, getting papers written on time, trying to fit in and feel accepted, and feeling that you are pulling a lot of weight and responsibility. There is the drama of comparing yourself to others and trying to measure up. There are relationship and friendship dramas, social media dramas, and rumors. Even a bad hair day can prove to be dramatic. It's how you manage those struggles that make the difference between real drama and unnecessary drama.

Drama queens tend to engage in and create unnecessary drama by making assumptions, misinterpreting things, or living by certain beliefs that keep them stuck and don't serve them in a positive way. They love to focus on everything that is wrong in the world instead of possibilities and what is right. They love to read things into stories that aren't yet written, and they love to exaggerate the truth. Drama queens throw in a little tragedy here and there, and a splash of color to make something more sensationalized. They love to make everything about them. The reason they behave this way is that they have a need that isn't being fulfilled, so they create situations to get the attention they crave. They are great actresses who love to play the part of the victim, and they love the attention they get from those who run to their aid. Even when something really great happens for the drama queen, she finds a way to twist it, manipulate it, and turn it into a tragedy because it wasn't enough in some way. They risk true friendships by always being dramatic and can find themselves alone because the constant drama eventually wears on those around them. The other hazard is that people will stop taking the drama queen seriously. You are too awesome for those kinds of results.

The teen diva deals with drama differently. She doesn't engage in unnecessary drama. Instead of adding to the drama and staying stuck in the problem, she chooses to focus on the solution. For example, if the teen diva is stressed out about finals, she steps back and looks at where the stress is coming from and figures out what she needs to do to minimize it in positive ways, so she can be successful (see "Who and What Are Influencing You"). She might need to set a boundary so she can have time and space for studying. She might need to change her study environment, lighting, or even do something as simple as changing her clothes, so she is more comfortable. Regardless, she solves the problem.

To be the drama queen dropout, you have to be willing to find the positives in a situation or the opportunities it presents, even if it's a hard lesson. The lesson teaches you how to do something better next time. You must choose to become someone who won't turn a small bump in the road into a complete road closure but will point out a way to get around the bump and back on track. You have to choose to become someone who is energizing and can give others involved a positive and encouraging boost.

There are positive ways of getting attention and negative ways of getting attention. The teen diva knows that the best ways of getting attention are to lose the crown, be positive, focused, inspired, and find effective solutions to the challenges. As a result, the teen diva becomes a magnet to success, great relationships, and life's positive experiences.

Characteristics of a Teen Diva	Characteristics of a Drama Queen
She is all about happiness, solutions, and success	She is *all* about crisis Everything is a hopeless disaster
She empowers others to be their best	She distracts others from being their best
She loves to solve problems—it helps her to grow, learn, and succeed	She loves to create problems
She lives and owns her truth	She exaggerates the truth

She is empathetic and supportive	She makes others' problems about her
She learns from the past and lives in the now	She lives in the past
She gets attention	She seeks attention
She is optimistic	She is pessimistic
Her glass is half full	Her glass is half empty
She lives balanced and in proportion	She blows things out of proportion
She's an energizer! You feel great when you are around her	She's an energy drainer
She directly says what she means—kindly	She has a passive attitude

Diva Tip:

If you have drama queen tendencies, don't panic! Every girl has them at times. Become self-aware and start making new and more diva-like attitude choices.

Journal It!

- *In what ways do you create drama in your life?*
- *In what ways do you invite drama into your life?*
- *How does the drama in your life affect your friendships/ relationships?*
- *In what ways do you attract positive attention in your life?*
- *In what ways do you attract negative attention in your life?*
- *What choices do you need to make to reduce the amount of drama in your life and become a drama queen dropout?*

Dantra

*I choose to lose the crown and become a drama queen dropout.
I know that life doesn't just happen to me; I participate in creating my own reality by the drama I engage in.*

Let it Go!

Let go of surrounding yourself with things that create drama in your life and instead surround yourself with the people and things that open up space for more happiness and success.

Double Diva Dare Ya!

To make a conscious choice not to engage in drama this week and instead engage with people and in things that create more happiness.

Power Tools: Which tools would you use and how would you use them?

- *Bill of rights*
- *Boundaries*
- *Character*
- *Choices*
- *Confidence*
- *Ownership*
- *Self-control*
- *Thought and intention*
- *Values*
- *Your voice*

What else will be helpful? _____

DQDRTW:

Drama queen dropouts rule the world

Conquering Fear

Fear tries to dictate your story—a story that hasn't been written yet. Snatch the pen back from fear and write your story beautifully. Be the author and illustrator of your life, diva girl. That's so diva!

—Diva

Regardless of what a person's fear revolves around, fear is very real. In a funny way, our fears try to care for us by holding and protecting us from the unknown and untruths like failure. Our fears try to dictate a story that hasn't yet been written. Fear becomes the author of your life rather than you writing the story you want to live and tell. It becomes one of the biggest blocks that prevent you from moving forward.

There are many questions we tend to ask ourselves when it comes to taking a risk and facing fear. "What if I screw up?" is the biggest of all. One big key to success and moving forward is to overcome whatever underlying fear you are experiencing and ask yourself, "What if I *do* succeed?" Better yet, "What will I do *when* I succeed?" When you give into the fictional story that fear tries to tell you, fear has all of your power. You've given it away. You are a diva of the world and powerfully courageous!

When you are ready to take action, your action will tear down the wall that fear put in front of you. On the other side of fear, you will find happiness, a sense of victory, and accomplishment. You are the diva in your life, and you will conquer all that you want to conquer when you are ready. Only you will know when you are ready. Know that you are worthy of success and everything wonderful. Put positive intentions out there for success, snatch back the pen and the power you gave to fear, and dare to write your story fearlessly.

Now, I want you to close your eyes and imagine your perfect diva world where fear doesn't exist. In your perfect diva world, nothing can hold you back from doing anything you want to do. What would you *divaly* accomplish?

Journal It!

- *What is your fear stopping you from achieving?*
- *What is your fear stopping you from becoming?*
- *What's going to happen if you don't challenge your fear?*
- *What's going to happen if you do challenge your fear?*
- *What's your fear really costing you emotionally, spiritually, academically, and in your relationships?*
- *If you could have a conversation with fear, what would you say? Hint—a power phrase might be handy.*
- *What are some resources that will help you challenge your fear and move forward? Who is your support?*

Dantra

I will not give my power to fear. I will not allow fear to dictate my today, my tomorrow, or my life. I am the author and illustrator of my life, and I will write my own story.
I am so diva!

Let it Go!
Let go of the lies that fear tells you.

Power Tools: Which tools would you use and how would you use them?

- *Assertiveness*
- *Bill of rights*
- *Boundaries*
- *Choices*
- *Confidence*
- *Language*
- *Power phrase*
- *Thought and intention*
- *Values*
- *Your voice*

What else will be helpful? _____

What Would a Diva Do?

The diva knows that Desdemona is fear's leader, and she is full of lies. The diva would counter Desdemona and fear by first exploring the truth behind the fear. For example, is your fear being dictated by Desdemona's lies? What is fear stopping you from becoming? Is it really true that you are doomed to fail? What makes that true for you? Then the teen diva would counter Desdemona and fear with a power phrase.

Power Phrase:

"Not today, fear! I am so diva, and I am going to write my beautiful and purposeful story—fearlessly! I've so got this!"

N2DF!:

Not today, fear!

Who and What Are Influencing You?

Only allow yourself to be under the influence of that which creates happiness and success for you—me!

—Diva

R emember how powerful I keep saying you are? You are powerful beyond belief, diva girl! Why is it then that sometimes we feel so powerless—like the world is happening to us and chasing us down as if we have some sort of a target on our backs? It's really not that we are being picked on by the world or that we are unlucky. Most of the time it's because we are unaware of the influences around us, as well as our power to change those influences and walk a more empowered path.

Most people think that influence comes from people, which it often does. I mean it's easy to fall under the influence of friends to dress a certain way, act a certain way, do certain things, and feel a certain way. However, there are many other ways that you can be influenced. Think about this: What influenced what you chose to wear today? Your mood! What influenced your mood? Perhaps how much sleep you had the night before. What influenced how much sleep you had? Perhaps staying up too late to do your homework because you struggled to focus. Why couldn't you focus? Perhaps you were worried about a friend, were wearing uncomfortable clothes while you studied, or were working with poor lighting in your room. I can go on and on with this saga, but I think you get the idea; influence shows up in many ways.

When you are upset or experiencing a lot of drama and stress, remember to ask yourself, "What is influencing this situation? What can I do to change it, so it works *for* me rather than *against* me?" When you experience success, ask yourself the same question—what influenced your success—and remember those things as you move forward.

Journal It!

Pick something that isn't working out the way you want it to.
- *What is influencing the result you are receiving? Is it a person, your environment, emotions, health, or attitude?*
- *What do you need to do to change that influence?*

Mantra

I have total control over the things that influence my success.

Let it Go!

Let go of suffering through stress and drama, and instead make the choice to be aware of your influences and create an atmosphere and attitude that set you up for success with ease and grace.

Double Diva Dare Ya!

To pick one thing that you've regularly struggled with and go on a journey to discover what is influencing the results you are receiving. Then do something to change the influence in a way that empowers you and sets you up for success.

Power Tools: Which tools would you use and how would you use them?

- *Assertiveness*
- *Boundaries*
- *Choices*
- *Confidence*
- *Gratitude*
- *Ownership*
- *Thought and intention*

What else will be helpful? _____

OUIOMID:

Only under the influence of my inner diva

The Teen Diva's Blues Busters

1. Be gentle with yourself. To beat the blues, you have to stop beating yourself up. Know that it's okay to feel down and allow yourself that space to rest quietly and reflect on what's got you down.

2. Reflect on what's really going on. What triggered your blues? Friendships? Relationships? Family matters? Pressures? Hormones? Academics?

3. Talk to someone. Saying things out loud can help sort things out. Choose someone you can trust, someone who won't make you feel bad about feeling bad.

4. Listen to inspiring music. Be careful what you put in your mind. Listen to things that inspire hope and light in you rather than something with darker, more depressing tones. Your brain is like a computer. It gets programmed with the messages you feed it.

5. Have a good cry. Tears are a blessing because they are teachers of love, forgiveness, compassion, and strength, and they remind us of what's really important to us. They remind us of the gifts and blessings in our lives.

6. Go for a nice long walk or engage in your favorite form of exercise. It's a stress reliever and will help you get more clarity. It also releases endorphins—happy hormones.

7. Laugh! Even if you have to force it. Think of something hilarious from your past and allow yourself to be fully back in that moment. This alone will get you giggling. Enjoy that moment of laughter.

8. Do something that you can relax and get lost in. Perhaps soak in a bubble bath, read a book, go for a walk, or sit outside and watch the clouds.

9. Write in a journal. Think of your journal as your best friend— someone you can talk to who won't judge you, blame you, cut you down, or make you feel worse. Your journal is a friend you can give all of your problems to and lighten the load that is weighing you down.

10. Express yourself creatively through dance, art, cooking, baking, writing, or whatever speaks to your heart.

11. Go into your heart and hear me, your inner diva—who knows your beautiful and bright truth better than anyone else—tell you how much I love you, respect you, and admire you.

12. If you are really stuck and can't get unstuck from your blues, then please see a licensed professional.

Journal It!

Try this: Think of your day and all that brought you down. As you journal about your day, start off with "Unfortunately," name what happened, follow that with "fortunately," and name a positive that came from it. For example, "Unfortunately, I dropped my books in front of a guy I really like and felt so embarrassed I could have died! Fortunately, he smiled at me and helped me pick them up. We chatted for a while, and I got to know him better."

Dantra

The blues and the tears that accompany them teach me what is important. They show me what I value, what I want, and what I don't want, and guide me to make different choices. That's so diva!

Let it Go!

Let go of whatever is not yours to hold on to that may be keeping you stuck in the blues. If someone said something unkind to you that made you sad, remember that when people are unkind, it's because they have had experiences that have brought them to a place of being unkind. It doesn't excuse them for their words or actions. It stops you from putting their "stuff" in your all. When you allow their cruelty to affect you, you are in a strange way accepting what they say as the truth, and by doing so you are giving away your power over your happiness. OMD! Don't give it away, diva girl! Let it go and send them a silent wish for compassion and kindness.

If you've made a mistake that you are beating yourself up for, find the lesson in the experience, apologize if you've wronged someone, forgive yourself, consider how you will take that lesson forward, and then let it go too.

Power Tools: Which tools would you use and how would you use them?

- *Bill of rights*
- *Compassion*
- *Gratitude*
- *Kindness*
- *Language*
- *Power phrase*

What else will be helpful? _____

The Teen Diva Values the Lessons She Learns from Her Mistakes

There is a jewel in every mistake we make if we allow it to empower us and light the way.

—Diva

M aking mistakes is kind of like hitting your funny bone. It hurts, and it's really not so funny! It's the stupid things we do that smart. Well, let's reframe that statement: it's the stupid things we do that make us smarter. Now, I'm not suggesting that you run out and do stupid things to get smarter. However, I want you to know that when you do make mistakes, they really do serve a purpose and should be celebrated because they help you to learn and grow. If you are not learning and growing, you are standing still in time, and time won't stand still for you. It will keep marching on with or without you. Believe me, there is a jewel in every mistake you make if you choose to acknowledge it and allow it to empower you.

Everyone makes mistakes. I promise you that even those people you see as perfect make mistakes too, and if you think they don't, it might be that they hide behind their mistakes by pointing their fingers at someone or something else—so *not* diva! Making a mistake and owning it takes a lot of courage and a dose of confidence. I mean, it's kinda scary thinking that if we admit to our mistakes, we might be judged as bad, stupid, or not good enough. Yuck! That's a big burden to carry. When I talk about owning mistakes, I'm talking about not placing blame on anyone or anything that may have influenced you. Remember, you have total control over the influences in your life.

Owning your mistakes means saying, "I allowed myself to be influenced by _____, and as a result, I really goofed up. I learned _____ from this mistake, and I know what I would choose differently next time." Now, if it were up to Desdemona, she would engage you in a totally different thought process by encouraging you to place blame on something or someone by saying, "If _____ hadn't done _____, I wouldn't have screwed up. It's their fault I am in trouble!" So *not* diva! You see the difference here? As a teen diva, you totally own your mistake, and as a result, you will find the precious jewel—your influence. When you know your influence, you become empowered to set a boundary that will help you make better choices going forward. Grab that jewel and put it in your tiara, princess!

Tip:

When you make a mistake, own it, learn from it, and allow yourself the time and space for reflection and self-forgiveness. Be kind and exercise self-compassion by not attaching dramatic and self-punishing meaning to your mistake. Find that golden jewel and wear it proudly.

Journal It!

Think of a mistake you've made that you're been holding on to.
- *What influenced you when you made that mistake?*
- *In what ways are you giving that mistake the power to define you now?*
- *What did you learn from that mistake, and how can you let it define you and empower you in a positive way?*
- *What was the greatest lesson you learned from that mistake?*
- *How can you apply that lesson to something positive in your future?*

Dantra

Mistakes are jewels in my crown. I can let them shine a light for me, empower me, and lead me on my path forward, or I can let them weigh me down. I am a diva, and I'm so shining my light!

Let it Go!

Let go of the need to be perfect, hide behind your mistakes, and blame external factors. You are in control of all that influences you. Own it, learn, and grow!

Double Diva Dare Ya!

To find a mistake you made recently. Consider what you need to own it and forgive it, and for it to empower you. Get excited about the positive ways the mistake is helping you to grow and succeed. Then let it empower you!

Power Tools: Which tools would you use and how would you use them?

- *Bill of rights*
- *Character*
- *Choices*
- *Compassion*
- *Confidence*
- *Gratitude*
- *Ownership*
- *Power phrase*

What else will be helpful? _____

ADGO:
Another diva growth opportunity

AJTLMW:
A jewel to light my way

Practice Being a Good Listener

To be fully heard, you must open your mind to hear what someone else is saying.

—Diva

Diva, you would think that listening would be as easy as riding a bike, but listening is one of the most difficult skills to master and, if not practiced, can be one of the greatest contributors to drama. Practicing good listening skills will help minimize conflicts and drama, or at least reduce the amount of drama you may feel. Lacking good listening skills causes the most misunderstandings and conflicts and, as a teenager, the most gossip and unnecessary drama.

When you are having a conversation, an argument, or a debate with a friend or family member, you might feel like you are not being fully heard or understood. How often do you want to scream (or do you scream), "O-M-D! You are *so* not listening to me!" How many times do others say the same to you? The trick to being fully heard is being willing to fully hear what someone else is saying, even if you disagree with what that person is saying.

This can be especially challenging because of the distractions going on in your own head like your emotions and judgments bubbling up. Or perhaps you start formulating what you are going to say next while the other person is still speaking. If you are caught up in emotions and how you will reply, you are not being fully present for the other person, and you are missing essential information.

Here are some tips for being fully present and making sure you stay open to understanding, as well as being understood:

◊ Drop the need to be right. Once you let go of the need to be right, you open your mind to hearing another perspective.

◊ Focus, focus, focus! Don't let anything distract you from listening to every word. Don't be distracted by things going on around you—maintain eye contact. *And* don't allow yourself to get distracted by formulating your response before the other person has finished speaking.

◊ Ask lots of questions! The more you ask, the more clarity you will gain.

◊ Don't invite GAIL into the conversation! She brings her gremlins, assumptions, interpretations, and limiting beliefs to conversations, and that just stirs up trouble.

◊ Repeat what the other person has said to make sure you are clear. That might sound something like this: "So what I heard you say is _____. Did I understand you correctly?"

◊ When you are comfortable, and it's your turn to respond, you might begin by saying, "I heard what you said and understand where you're coming from. Now I'd like to share where I am coming from too."

135

◊ If you get interrupted, use your boundaries and say, "I gave you time and space to speak your point of view without interrupting, and I'd appreciate it if you would give me the same courtesy and not interrupt me. Please let me finish."

When you practice active listening, you listen to understand and to find solutions. Active listeners focus on win-win. Everyone wants to be heard and understood. Everyone also wants to feel validated for believing what he or she does. Validation doesn't mean you are telling others that you agree with their viewpoint or that they are right. It means you are acknowledging that they feel the way they do and that their feelings are real. For example, "Of course you feel frustrated. Based on what has happened to you in the past, I don't blame you for feeling that way. But I'd really like you to hear me and understand why I feel the way I do too."

Journal It!

- *How often do you not feel like you are being heard?*
- *When you feel like you are not being heard, how do you respond?*
- *When you are in an argument or a debate with someone, what are you thinking or doing while they are sharing their viewpoint? How does that get in the way of you actively listening?*
- *What is it about you that keeps you from hearing another perspective?*

- *How often do you feel the need to be right? Why is being right important to you? How do you benefit from needing to be right?*
- *What does needing to be right cost you?*
- *What would it take for you to be more present and more open to another perspective?*

Dantra

Everyone has different ideas—not right or wrong, different. The more I listen, the more information I gain, the more I learn, and the more I understand.

Let it Go!

Let go of the need to be right and open yourself up to different perspectives, new ideas, and more possibilities. Seek a win-win!

Double Diva Dare Ya!

To be mindful the next time you are having a discussion or an argument, and refrain from interrupting or being distracted by your formulated response. Be 100 percent present!

Power Tools: Which tools would you use and how would you use them?

- *Character*
- *Choices*
- *Compassion*
- *Language*
- *Ownership*
- *Self-control*
- *Values*

*What else will be helpful?*_____

Being Balanced and Managing Your Time

Balance isn't something you find; it's something you create.

—Diva

Too often teen girls feel like they have too much on their plate and need to find balance. These years are full of activities, responsibilities, academics, events, and relationships that can leave you feeling like you are off balance and stressed. It's normal! What I want you to understand is that balance isn't something to be "found"—it's something you create and have total control over by making different and better choices. If you are feeling off-kilter—like there's not enough time in the day to do everything (including not having any time for yourself!)—you have given away your diva power to someone or something, probably Desdemona. She loves to interfere, make you overextend yourself, and deplete your energy!

Okay, so there are twenty-four hours in a day, and when you think about it, that's a lot of time to play with. Awesome! It's what you choose to do with that time that will make a great difference for you.

139

Desdemona will try to get you to overextend yourself and block you from achieving, but you can counter her by being intentional with your time and manage it well. As a diva, I highly encourage you to consider everything that needs to be done in that time frame, including eight hours for sleeping—you need your rest. That leaves you with sixteen hours to do what you need and desire to do. If you manage your time well, you will create balance and ideally have some of that time for self-care, such as exercise, reading, relaxing, spirituality, or whatever rejuvenates you and positively nourishes your spirit. You've *so* got this!

I want you to create your perfect day. Apply this concept to each season (school year, summer, winter break, weekends, etc.). Before you begin, consider the following:

◊ There are things you can't change like going to school, sports, extra activities, etc. What are the things you can't change? Block out time for them.

◊ What do you need to carve out time for that is in line with your top values? For example, if spending time with family is essential for you, make sure to block out your ideal time with your family.

◊ Make time for what matters most: taking care of yourself. You can't give what you don't have, so make sure you carve out enough time for self-care, whatever that is for you. Examples of self-care might be exercise, quiet time, and other things that nourish your spirit.

◊ Are you a morning person? Do you have a lot of energy when you get home from school? Do you feel most energized after you exercise? Think about when you have the most energy and block out that time for the things that require the most thought and attention from you.

There will be times in life when you have to be a bit more flexible to accommodate random things like a celebration of some sort, a school meeting, a crisis, or a social event. However, the key is to remember that you have total control over how you manage your time. You are a DITCH!

When Desdemona is influencing your time and balance, you will feel

◊ anxious,

◊ irritable,

◊ hopeless,

◊ depressed,

◊ angry,

◊ paralyzed by the amount you have to do and the lack of time to do it, and

◊ like a victim to time and responsibilities.

When I, your inner diva, am influencing your time, you will feel

◊ fearless,

◊ confident,

◊ happy,

◊ excited,

◊ energized,

◊ accomplished,

◊ successful,

◊ assured (like you've *totally* got this!),

◊ like things are effortless,
◊ like nothing can stop you,
◊ totally in control to create your day and successes throughout the day, and
◊ totally awesome!

You will celebrate your accomplishments!

Journal It!

- *What do you say yes to that makes you feel off balance?*
- *What boundary do you need to set to create more balance for yourself?*
- *How do you feel about the way you manage your time?*
- *What changes can you choose to make to manage your time better, create more balance, and reduce stress for yourself?*

Mantra

I am in total control of managing my time and creating balance for myself.

Let it Go!

Let go of overextending yourself and depleting your energy. Manage your time and activities in a way that energizes you instead!

Double Diva Dare Ya!

To reschedule or remove things from your schedule that inhibit you from being balanced. There is a time for everything, and sometimes the time is later.

Power Tools: Which tools would you use and how would you use them?

- *Assertiveness*
- *Boundaries*
- *Choices*
- *Language*
- *Ownership*
- *Thought and intention*

What else will be helpful? _____

BITWOYD:

Balance is the way of the diva

Chapter 4

Body Image for the Teen Diva

Stop Comparing Yourself to Others

Only when you choose to stop taking the worst parts of yourself and comparing them to the best parts of others will you be able to see your true beauty.

—Diva

irror, mirror on the wall, who is the fairest of them all? *You* are! In the movie *Snow White*, the queen looks into the mirror and asks this famous question. The magic mirror replies, "Famed is thy beauty, Majesty. But, behold, a lovely maid I see. Rags cannot hide her gentle grace. Alas, she is more fair than thee." Snow White's beauty could not be hidden behind the rags she wore or the status she held as a maid. Her beauty radiated from her lovely character and kind spirit.

Sweet and pretty diva, the human body is a beautiful work of art regardless of if it is tall, short, heavy, thin, freckled, pale, or dark skinned. We were all created differently, all with beautifully unique features and a captivating presence (when we allow it to be seen!). Yet, just like the queen, we tend to look to outside validation that we are beautiful. Or perhaps we even look in the mirror and go through the big *but* syndrome. Instead of admiring our great features, we say, "My waist might be small, *but* my butt is too big." Or "My butt is cute, *but* my chest isn't filled out like Jennifer's." Or "*But* I wish I had a more curvy figure like Alexa instead of the straight figure I have."

Why do we girls do that? Why do we look in the mirror and intentionally take the worst parts of ourselves and compare them to the best parts of someone else? You are *so* not being fair to yourself, and you're allowing Desdemona to be the reflection in your mirror and not me, your inner diva. I would be telling you, "Hot damn and *shazam!*" and then direct your attention to your best feature, encouraging you to make your best features stand out.

I have to tell you, sweet diva, the eyes are the most beautiful part of the human body and also the most deceptive. They are the most beautiful because they are like a looking glass into the soul and reveal so much. They reveal who we are, what we are about, and what kind of mood we are in. They sparkle when we are feeling our best, shed tears when we are sad, and grow intense when we are angry or at our worst. The reason our eyes are deceptive is that they influence us to judge what we perceive as flawed, and this alone robs us from seeing what is truly beautiful. The eyes can create separation because they judge whether or not things are good enough based on what is *seen*, not on what is real and true in us and others. It's really no wonder that so many girls struggle with body image and insecurity.

I want you to understand something vital. Your body isn't what makes you shine; it's only a shell that carries your truest and most beautiful self—your character and your spirit. When you walk into a room, genuine people won't look at your body; that's not what catches their attention. They won't remember what you wore, how you styled your hair, or the size of your butt. What they will remember is how you made them feel with your captivating spirit. They will see and feel your essence, and they will always remember how you made them feel by radiating your truest beauty. There are no perfect bodies out there; they are all perfectly imperfect. And, you are *be-you*-tiful because you are unique and captivating in your own diva way.

A word of caution: If people criticize or shame you for your body, know that they are under the influence of Desdemona. Do not entertain them by reacting or allowing them to make you feel less than you really are—small, insignificant, and bad about yourself. You have a choice. You can allow that to happen, and in return, they win and steal your power and happiness. Or you can recognize that they are not worth giving your time, attention, or emotions to and not engage in the drama they are trying to create for you. Remain confident and allow yourself to shine for those who care about and appreciate you for the uniquely beautiful and radiant young lady and spirit that you are.

Journal It!

- *What parts of your body do you love the most?*
  - ° *What is it about those areas of your body that you love?*
  - ° *How do those areas contribute to your character, interests, and/or personality?*
  - ° *What do you value most about those parts of your body? How do they support you? Make a big list!*
- *What parts of your body are you most unhappy about?*

○ *Who or what has influenced you not to like those parts of your body?*
○ *Who are you comparing yourself to?*
○ *If you are comparing yourself to models or the definitions that society has given you about beauty and success, do you really believe it to be true? Why? What makes it true for you?*
○ *If you didn't point out those flaws to others, would they notice them? Don't plant weeds!*
○ *What is it about those parts of your body that make you uncomfortable?*
○ *How do those parts of your body serve you positively?*
○ *What would you have to change to become comfortable with those parts of your body?*
○ *How would those changes affect the way you would show up every day?*

• *Now have a conversation with your body. I know, I know, this sounds kinda weird, but trust me! You might even find yourself having fun and giggling. Your body tells a story. If you were to thank your body what would you say? Why? What story does it tell? What victory has your body brought you? What lesson has your body taught you? How has your body inspired you or helped you succeed in some way? In what ways has your body protected you? Express your gratitude for your body.*

- *Here are some other things to consider when it comes to your body image:*
  - *When you look in the mirror and focus your attention on your (perceived) flaws, what does that rob you of seeing?*
  - *How can you bring out your best features more so you are less insecure about your (perceived) worst features?*

Dantra

I love and embrace my perfectly imperfect body. My body is a shell that holds who I truly am and carries my truest beauty, my captivating spirit.

Let It Go!

Let go of being so unfair to yourself by taking the (perceived) worst parts of yourself and comparing them to the best parts of other girls.

Double Diva Dare Ya!

To look in the mirror for ten minutes and focus on the parts of yourself that you think are beautiful. Do not allow your eyes to move to the places you don't like. If your eyes and mind wander to a place of negativity and self-shaming, send those thoughts away. Dismiss them by saying, "not today" and return your attention to your best features.

Create your own diva body-image power phrase:

_____

_____

Power Tools: Which tools would you use and how would you use them?

- *Compassion*
- *Confidence*
- *Gratitude*
- *Kindness*
- *Language*
- *Power phrase*

What else will be helpful? _____

HDAS!:

Hot damn and shazam*!*

Eating Disorders Will Eat You Up!

Nourish your body, mind, and spirit with my love—always.

—Diva

While comparing ourselves to others is never a good idea and totally counterproductive because we are all born beautifully different, it is natural to some degree. It's natural until you start taking such drastic measures to achieve a (perceived) perfect image that you are doing your body harm. There is a lot of pressure out there to have the perfect body, but I am here to educate and tell you that if you are considering more extreme ways to achieve your (perceived) perfect body, I want you to speak with a trusted adult and get help immediately. Please see the resources listed at the back of this book.

Did you know that your body isn't fully developed until you are twenty-five years old? Crazy, right? But it's true. It's a lot of work for your body to grow up and develop into a healthy adult, and it requires a lot of nourishment and care on your part. When your body is not properly nourished and rested, experiences trauma, or is exposed to toxic substances, your entire system will become out of whack. I want you to be aware of the harm that eating disorders can inflict on you and your future. I cannot sugarcoat any of this, and frankly, that's not my job as your inner diva. My job is to protect you and guide you into a bright future. My job is to remind you of how loved, beautiful, and purposeful you are and always will be.

The two eating disorders I am going to talk about deprive your body of nutrients. These two disorders are anorexia and bulimia, and they share common characteristics. While the method behind each is slightly different, both of them cause girls to become obsessed with calories, body image, and weight. And both cause serious harm by depriving the body of what it needs to grow and thrive. When you deprive your body of necessary nutrients and care, it will shut down. Literally, it will shut down. And may not restart.

Causes and Effects of Eating Disorders
Cause: Desdemona!

◊ She convinces girls that they will never measure up to what society says a beautiful and successful teenage girl should be. The funny thing is society doesn't know us as individuals, so it has *no* clue that we cannot possibly fit into the same mold of beauty and success. We are all built uniquely and beautifully different in every way.

◊ She perpetually points out girls' flaws and causes them to obsess about never being liked or accepted unless they are perfect in every way.

◊ She makes them believe they have to put undue pressure on themselves to be perfect that she robs them of any joy they could be experiencing in life.

Effects:

◊ Deteriorating health
◊ Hormone imbalances
◊ Stunted bone growth
◊ Messed-up reproductive cycles (periods)
◊ Infertility
◊ Rotting teeth
◊ Depression
◊ Heart problems
◊ Inability to focus
◊ Weakened muscle and bone density
◊ Death

Power Tool

See a licensed professional *who specializes in eating disorders.*

Models and the Media's Measuring Stick

You can't live up or down to things that are not real—
things that don't even exist.

—Diva

With all of the pictures of models with perfect bodies, clothes, and makeup swarming around us, it's no wonder girls are so insecure about their self-image and run themselves into a frenzy trying to find the best solution or magic pill for perfection. What those pictures don't reveal are all of the tools used to touch up the models, so they look perfect or the health sacrifices those models have to make to be perceived as perfect. The truth is that you cannot live up to or down to things that don't exist.

Models have some of the toughest jobs out there. I mean it would be pretty difficult to do a job where you can't be 100 percent yourself. They are subjected to restrictions and constant criticism. They are judged by what the eyes see, not by anything that can be felt or inspired by the heart. Can you imagine not being able to eat what you want, or obsessing over a number on a scale, or having people constantly telling you that you're not enough or you need to be better—just to be touched up after the photo shoot is over?

Models have to make so many sacrifices to do what they do, and they have to put on a good face for the enjoyment of the public, perfect strangers. Here's the thing, sweet diva: They do this because it's their job. It's their job to inspire you with fashion trends and makeup, and hopefully with information that helps you develop an individual style to match your body style, face shape, skin coloring, eye coloring, hair type, and so on. Your job as a teenager is to discover who you are and what works for you, and live happily, enjoying and appreciating that you are uniquely beautiful. Your job is to engage in things that help you define for yourself what beauty and success are and then step fully into the spirited, unique, and beautiful young woman you are meant to be.

Journal It!

- *What model do you gravitate toward and admire the most? Why?*
- *In what ways are you similar to that model?*
- *In what ways are you uniquely different?*
- *Do the messages you get from this model inspire you to step into your unique brand of beauty, or do they make you feel like you don't measure up?*
- *If you were a model, how would you want teenage girls to see you? What empowering message would you send to teenage girls who struggle with body image?*

Dantra

Mirror, mirror on the wall, I am beautiful. I am unique. I am strong. I am enough. I am a teen diva!

Let It Go!

Let go of the need to be just like anyone else. You were born to be uniquely beautiful and purposeful.

Double Diva Dare Ya!

To pay a compliment to someone who is struggling with self-image. Seek out your favorite part of this person's style, compliment her, and remind her of her own unique beauty and how that makes her special and admirable.

Power Tools: Which tools would you use and how would you use them?

- *Compassion*
- *Confidence*
- *Gratitude*
- *Kindness*
- *Language*
- *Power phrase*

What else will be helpful? _____

SIMODS:

Stepping into my own diva style

Chapter 5

Friends and Frenemies for the Teen Diva

What Does It Mean to Be a Good Friend?

A true friend will hold up the mirror of yesterday's beauty and successes for you when you don't like the reflection you are seeing today. That's so diva!

—Diva

These are the teen diva's rules on being a good friend:

◊ Be the kind of friend you want to have.

◊ Set the same expectations for yourself that you have for the qualities you desire in a friend—walk your talk.

◊ Be there, even if it's a silent presence. You have no idea how powerful your presence can be even when you are not talking.

◊ Be happy for your friends and celebrate their successes.

◊ Be loyal.

◊ Keep your commitments; don't flake out.

◊ Listen.

◊ Empower your friends to be the best they can be.

◊ Don't hold grudges; forgive and let go.

◊ Be honest, even if it hurts.

◊ Don't let them walk around with boogers hanging out of their nose or toilet paper hanging from their backside.

◊ Stand up for your friends.

◊ Be trustworthy and keep their secrets, unless their secret is intended to be harmful to themselves or others.

◊ Create a safe space for them to be themselves.

◊ Be respectful.

◊ Don't make them feel bad about feeling bad.

◊ Don't take on their stuff, but help them sort through their stuff.

◊ Make sure you give at least as much as you take, and don't keep score.

◊ Be unconditional. The sisterhood of divas (SOD) is for better and worse. Divas help keep other divas in check.

◊ Hold up the mirror of yesterday's beauty and successes when they don't like the reflection they see.

◊ Remind them of their beauty and all that makes them special.

Journal It!

- *Who are my best friends?*
- *How do we bring out the best in each other?*
- *What are our common values that make our friendship really work?*
- *In what ways do we help each other to be our best selves?*
- *In what ways do we keep each other safe and free to be ourselves?*
- *In what ways do we support each other in making good choices?*

Dantra

I will be the kind of friend to others that I want for myself. I will choose to spend time with people who share similar values and interests.

Let It Go!

Let go of the need to be just like anyone else. You were born to be uniquely beautiful and purposeful.

Double Diva Dare Ya!

To send a thoughtful note or gift to a friend for no other reason than to remind the person how special he or she is to you and why you appreciate this friend so much.

Power Tools: Which tools would you use and how would you use them?

- Boundaries
- Character
- Choices
- Compassion
- Values

What else will be helpful? _____

SOD:

Sisterhood of divas

Choosing Friends

Choosing friends is like choosing a new pair of shoes. You want them to be comfortable, supportive, fun, sassy, complement your style, and walk well with you on your life journey.

—Diva

Guess what, diva? Here is another thing you have total power over: the friends you choose! As you move through the teenage years, you will most likely start attending larger schools, which means you will be growing your friendships. You might even question where you fit in and where you want to fit in. It can be overwhelming and feel like you are lost in a sea of faces. This is perfectly normal. The good news is that you have an entire sea of faces to choose from. The tricky thing is knowing what you want in a friend and picking the right friends to hang around with—people who have your best interests at heart.

The teen diva will attract what she wants when she surrounds herself with the right people and keeps her eyes on her future visions and dreams. As you are faced with deciding what kind of friends you want to choose, I want you to keep a few things in mind. First, remember to keep your passions, goals, interests, and future visions in the front of your mind. What do you want to be? Who do you want to be? What's your big dream? What do you want your future to look like? I know, I know, this might sound weird since we are talking about choosing friends, but stick with me here. Your friends, if you have true friends, will not let you make poor choices, will share similar values and interests, and will keep you on track for a good future. They will hold your vision for you and keep you moving toward all you want in the future. And you will do the same for them. Keep those in mind who have the best influence on you. You also want to be sure to surround yourself with those who hold you accountable and cheer you on.

Here are some ways to know the difference between friends and frenemies.

True Diva Friends	Frenemies
Brag about you to others	Make you look bad in front of others
Are trustworthy	Don't keep your secrets
Are there for you to support you and celebrate the good and bad	Only show up when *they* need something
Are always kind	Bully you and then try to convince you that they were "just kidding"

Remind you of your strengths and divaness	Focus on your weaknesses
Are considerate and kind	Are rude and inconsiderate
Will warn you at the edge of making bad choices and remind you that you are so diva	Challenge you to do things that are not in your best interest
Will always stand up for you	Don't stand up for you

Diva tip on choosing friends:

When you surround yourself with friends who bring out the best in you and make you feel like you can do and be anything, then you *will* be able to do anything and live your best diva life. Remember, how you think and feel influences how you act.

Journal It!

Write out all of the characteristics that are important to you in friendships, for example, spiritual, honest, trustworthy, funny, athletic, playful, grateful, and studious.

- *Define what a good friend means to you. How do they make you feel?*

- *Where can you go to surround yourself with people who match your values, interests, and desires in a friend?*
- *What are the "must have" matching values for you in a friendship?*

Dantra

When I surround myself with people who match my values and complement my character, I feel safe in making good choices and staying on track. I acknowledge that the expectations I have of my friends I must also have of myself. That's so diva!

Let it Go!

Let go of your fear of meeting new people or not being accepted. When you choose people who have similar interests and values, you will almost certainly be accepted. If not, there is a clash in values, and you probably don't want that person influencing what matters most to you anyway. Go fish again in that sea of possibilities.

Double Diva Dare Ya!

To make a list of ten people you think would be a great fit for a friend—people you have things in common with and people who share the same morals and values. Now pick one who really resonates with you, and strike up a conversation with that person. Use your conversational skills and ask lots of questions, pay him or her a compliment, and ask if he or she wants to hang out sometime or go to an activity you share an interest in. Lastly, and super important to remember, have fun!

Power Tools: Which tools would you use and how would you use them?

- Assertiveness
- Character
- Choices
- Compassion
- Confidence
- Kindness
- Language
- Values

What else will be helpful? _____

DLOA:

Diva's laws of attraction

Who's Your Enabler?

The choices you make today say a lot about your character and will impact the person you are to become tomorrow.

—Diva

aking the choice to be empowered and to empower others to be their best is one of the greatest commitments you can make to yourself, to those around you, and to your purposeful contributions to this world. Remember, divas are confident. They bring out the best in themselves and others. However, it also takes a confident person to call you out when you are doing things that are not in your best interest. If someone isn't calling you out in an effort to help you be your best, that person is helping you to be your worst, and it may be time to weed your garden.

Validation demonstrates support. So, when you feel a certain way about something, a friend might say, "Of course you feel that way given what you've been through," thereby supporting your feelings. Sometimes we need validation. In fact, validation is really important and can be empowering and motivating. When you empower others, you help them to be their best and accomplish their goals and dreams. You energize them and remind them that with their unique gifts, strengths, and abilities, they've totally got this! That's *so* diva!

Imagine that you are standing with someone at the foot of an apple tree. The person you are with says, "Wow, that apple looks like it might have a worm in it, but it's more within reach. I'd eat that one because it might be too uncomfortable for you to stretch and grab the good apples a little higher." Sometimes we get confused between motivating, empowering, and enabling. Empowering helps people to be their best and achieve the best, while enabling gives people permission to be at their worst by allowing them to live below their potential and abilities. Enabling gives people permission to live by and use excuses as a crutch. It keeps people stuck in a victim mentality that says this is as good as it will ever get, and it's not worth the effort to try. Who do you think is driving that apple cart? Yep, you guessed it: Desdemona! She loves to keep girls living small.

I want you to be sure that you always empower yourself and all of those you encounter. I want you to set the tone in your environment and be the example that with a little hard work, the right attitude, and some empowering support, anything is possible. I also want you to be aware of those in your life who give you permission to not live to the best of your abilities, those who keep you small. Be aware of those who say, "I'm not sure you can do it; it's going to be pretty tough." If you have those people in your life, you may want to have a conversation with them and practice your assertive skills. Perhaps set a boundary. They may not realize they are hurting you. If they continue to keep you living small, weed your garden or minimize how much time you spend with them so you can stay energized and move forward toward a bright future.

The diva leads you to be supportive and empowering to others. She might say things like this:

◊ O-M-D! It's totally understandable that you feel the way you do. What are your options to change the situation, so you'll feel better? How can I support you?

◊ With your talent, you've *so* got this!

◊ I get where you might feel stretched, but I totally believe in your ability to accomplish whatever you put your mind to. You've got what it takes, and I know you're gonna rock it!

Desdemona will try to enable you to be your worst by making you second-guess yourself and convincing you that you aren't enough:

◊ Wow, it's not going to be easy for you. Are you sure you're up for it?

◊ Not everyone can be a success. Maybe this isn't what you are supposed to be doing.

◊ You have to be pretty amazing to get into that school. I just want you to be prepared in case you are disappointed.

Journal It!

- *Who in your life empowers and stretches you to be your best?*
- *In what ways do you empower and stretch others to be their best?*
- *Who in your life enables you to not try as hard? Who keeps you small?*

- *How can you help them understand the difference and set a boundary, so they have your best interests at heart?*

Dantra
I am a diva. I am empowered. I empower others.

Let it Go!
Let go of the influence of those who keep you living small. Focus instead on what is possible, and know that you are capable of all that speaks to and is aligned with your heart.

Double Diva Dare Ya!
To commit to yourself and those around you that you will empower and be empowered.

Power Tools: Which tools would you use and how would you use them?

- Assertiveness
- Bill of rights
- Boundaries
- Character
- Choices
- Confidence
- Language
- Ownership

- Power phrase
- Self-control
- Thought and intention
- Values
- Your voice

What else will be helpful? _____

DED:

Divas empowering divas

Individuality Doesn't Always Clique

If you don't click, then don't clique.

—Diva

One of the most basic human needs is the need to belong. This desire grows in intensity during the teenage years when you are trying to more deeply step into your identity and explore new friendships and activities. Everyone has a desire to be a part of something, and it's essential to your well-being to feel that you have a place where you belong. But ... here's the thing: it's even more important to belong to things that bring out the best in you and don't leave you feeling lonely, stifled, and without your identity when you are a part of them.

Cliques can be so appealing like being a part of an elite club. But, depending on the group, they can also be confining and stifling, leaving you with limited opportunities for other relationships and experiences. Too often, girls lose their identity because they have taken on and been boxed into the group identity. Within the group, they are expected to dress, talk, and behave in a certain way, and only hang out with other kids in the clique. Can you see that this could lead you to even more confusion, as you are trying to figure out and define who you are and what you want during these years? If you get in with the wrong clique, you might find that you are falling under the influence and definitions of others, and you might feel like you are losing the freedom to create and dream for yourself.

High school is full of cliques, some good and some not so good. It isn't wrong to be in a clique or have a group that you primarily hang out with—if it works for you. Remember, we are not a one-size-fits-all model. We are made different and have different needs. However, consider this as you explore friendships and cliques: Make sure you choose groups and friends who don't put you into a box of their ideals of who you are, who you should become, and whom you can or cannot hang out with. Surround yourself with people who allow you creative freedom to be yourself and become the person you want to be. Make sure you are always a part of groups involving divas supporting divas.

Journal It!

- *Are you in a clique? If so, how does that clique inspire you and encourage you to be your best?*
- *In what ways do you feel empowered by that clique?*
- *In what ways do you feel limited by that clique?*
- *How does that clique discriminate against you or others?*
- *Is that clique open to new friendships and opportunities, or is it exclusive?*

- *In what ways does your clique support your interests, goals, dreams, and happiness?*
- *What do you need more of that you are not getting from a closed group of friends? Propose ways to meet those needs.*
- *If you are not a part of a clique and have no interest in becoming part of a clique but instead have many different friends, write about where you meet your friends, what interests you share, and your ideal social situation in high school.*

Dantra

I am so my own individual and will not be stifled by others requiring me to conform to their ideals of who I should or shouldn't be. I choose to engage with those who give me the freedom to experience many opportunities. Boom! That's so diva!

Let it Go!

Let go of the need to be just like everyone else to fit in. You were born to shine brightly and be seen for the amazing diva you are! Set an individuality trend.

Double Diva Dare Ya!

Start your own teen diva empowerment group and invite people into your group who share similar interests and have similar values. Invite other girls who might benefit from the group—girls who could use other people to set the example of good friends with good values. Invite girls who want to become positive change setters at your school, and start

a new trend. Create a group where you don't have closed doors but rather a safe space where everyone is welcome, providing they follow some simple house rules like these:

- *We are all here to support each other and to keep each other strong and safe in our own individual identity, our goals, and on the right path.*
- *All in the group empower each other and keep each other positive.*
- *When you don't exclude people from being in your life, they will include you in theirs. Start a new trend; it will be contagious! That's so diva!*

Power Tools: Which tools would you use and how would you use them?

- *Assertiveness*
- *Boundaries*
- *Character*
- *Choices*
- *Gratitude*
- *Kindness*
- *Language*
- *Values*

What else will be helpful? _____

DSD:

Divas supporting divas

Weeding Your Garden

Give me that Weed Eater, a shovel, and some new seeds.
I've so got this!

—Diva

iva girl, springtime is about renewal and fresh starts. It's the time of year when plants and trees wake up from their dormant state and when fresh gardens are planted. Your life is your garden of variety at every season. How it is nourished and grows is entirely up to you.

Gardens require careful planning, constant care, and consideration. For a garden to thrive, it requires weeding out the toxic to allow for healthy new growth and beautiful blooms. Often in the garden of life the weeds that are choking us can represent many things. Perhaps you have a friend who is constantly negative and always brings you down. Perhaps you have people in your life who pressure you to do things that you know are not in your best interest and that might harm your future, mind, body, or spirit. Perhaps you are dating someone who doesn't show you respect and makes you feel bad about yourself—

someone who brings out the worst in you instead of the best. Maybe you have a habit or an attitude that you want to change. You might even have a memory of a bad experience that is holding you back from fresh, new experiences. These represent the weeds in your life. Great news! *You* have the power to pluck the weeds and plant new seeds so you can thrive and grow! *You* get to choose how to nourish your garden of life.

Grow your garden of life beautifully, remembering that you get to choose what you can plant. Plant your own variety of seeds and plant them positively and strategically, so they feed your future. Nourish your garden with the things that are most important to you, things that make you come alive, and rid your garden of the negativity and toxins that prevent you from healthy growth.

Journal It!

- *What weeds in your life are inhibiting your growth and happiness? Is it an attitude or habit of yours? Is it another person who keeps you small?*
- *What is making you hold on to this negativity?*
- *Take that thought and make the choice to let it go. Change that thought in a way that will work for you rather than against you.*
- *What is holding on to this negativity—this weed— costing you in your life, relationships, school, attitude, and so forth?*

Dantra

Give me that Weed Eater, shovel, and new seeds. I've so got this!

Let it Go!

Let go of the negativity that inhibits your happiness, productivity, visions, and success. Don't forget also to let go of any habits or attitudes in your life that cause you to be the weed in someone else's garden.

Double Diva Dare Ya!

To choose one weed in your garden that is inhibiting your happiness and growth. Most often, the weed is there because of a choice you made. Think about how you want to acknowledge that weed and choose differently going forward. What choice are you going to make about this weed?

Power Tools: Which tools would you use and how would you use them?

- *Assertiveness*
- *Bill of rights*
- *Boundaries*
- *Character*
- *Choicesa*
- *Gratitude*
- *Ownership*
- *Thought and intention*
- *Values*

What else will be helpful? _____

WYG:

Weed your garden

Tip:

Remember, happiness is not a future destination. Happiness can be achieved now and is available to you at all times. You have to choose it and make choices (with the end in mind) that will create happiness for you and nourish your garden of life. When you choose happiness and weed your garden of toxic things, the garden will grow beautifully, and you will find great success in all you do. Happiness creates success. Plant all the things that make you happy in your garden.

Chapter 6

Dating and the Teen Diva

Understanding Healthy and Unhealthy Relationships

I am in complete control of my half of every relationship I am in.

—Diva

Let's do some girl talking! Relationships are a necessary part of living a healthy life. While we are totally into the girl-talk thing in this section and focused on romantic relationships, I want you to remember that the same principles and information apply to all kinds of relationships, whether they're with friends, parents, siblings, teachers, and so on.

It's *so* exciting to move into the teenage years, where you are taking more interest in romantic relationships and spending your time with someone who makes you feel special and beautiful—someone who makes you feel like a princess, go to events with, and show off. I know, you're waiting for the big *but* to come along, so here goes. I'll make it quick so we can get to the good stuff sooner than later.

But to be in a healthy relationship, you first need to understand the difference between a healthy relationship and an unhealthy relationship.

Believe it or not, your partner can make you feel like a princess, but you still can be in an unhealthy relationship. I want you to understand the difference between healthy and unhealthy relationships because it's my job as your inner diva to keep you safe and feeling the best about yourself.

In healthy relation-ships, the teen diva	In unhealthy relation-ships, the teen diva
feels respected;	feels disrespected;
sets boundaries that are respected;	has no boundaries, or boundaries are crossed and disrespected;
feels a great sense of self-worth;	feels bad about herself;
feels heard and is *totally* comfortable speaking her mind;	feels unworthy of being heard and is uncomfortable speaking up;
is balanced between her relationship, school, friends, family, activities, etc.;	feels dominated and isn't "allowed" to have balance;
is comfortable being her unique and fabulous self;	feels like she has to become someone else;

feels comfortable and safe expressing herself;	feels fear when expressing herself;
is encouraged to be her best;	doesn't feel supported;
doesn't worry about abuse and violence;	fears for her safety;
feels her privacy is respected; and	worries that her partner will break into her cell phone, read her texts, snoop, talk to people behind her back, etc.; and
feels that sexual boundaries are respected (if it is a sexual relationship).	feels pressured to do things she is not comfortable with. For example, "If you really cared about me you would …" Note: If they really cared about you, they would respect your feelings and want you to feel comfortable and safe.

In a nutshell, healthy relationships are based entirely on trust and respect. When I talk about respect I mean that boundaries are honored, there is a willingness to compromise, and both individuals show consideration for each other and feel safe physically and emotionally. In addition, you are free to be yourself and still maintain balance with everything that is important to you, such as schoolwork, your spirituality, spending time with family and friends, and taking time for yourself. Uh-oh, here comes another big *but*. But before you can expect anyone else to respect you, you must first respect yourself.

I want you to understand that when something causes you pain or discomfort, whether emotional or physical, and you don't feel you have the power to stop it—or even worse, that you believe you deserve it—there is a *big* problem. If this is the case, know that you *never* deserve to be treated in a way that causes you pain, and you *do* have the power to stop it by using your voice. Talk to a trusted friend, teacher, adult, counselor, or spiritual advisor. Also, reference the back of this book where you will find a list of helplines you can call.

Journal It!

- *Describe your ideal relationship.*
- *List the people in your life with whom you have the healthiest relationships.*
- *What makes them healthy?*
- *What relationships in your life increase your self-worth? Add value?*
- *What relationships in your life are the unhealthiest? What makes them unhealthy for you? Why?*
- *What are you settling for or putting up with? Why?*

- What core morals and values must match up in your relationships?
- Are you in a relationship for the right or wrong reason? What are those reasons?

Dantra
A healthy relationship will add joy and value to my life, bringing out the best in me. I am worthy of healthy relationships and choose to engage with those I feel safe with and comfortable around.

Let it Go!
Let go of the need to become a character other than who you truly are in a relationship. There is a reason the person liked you in the first place. Stay true to who you are!

Double Diva Dare Ya!
To seek out relationships based on values, morals, common interests, and the things that increase your self-worth.

Power Tools: Which tools would you use and how would you use them?

- *Assertiveness*
- *Bill of rights*
- *Boundaries*
- *Character*
- *Choices*

- *Language*
- *Ownership*
- *Self-control*
- *Values*
- *Your voice*

What else will be helpful? _____

LALM:
Leaving a little mystery

DDCR:
Dating divas command respect

Tips for Dating with Confidence

◊ Do something before you go out that puts you in a contagiously awesome mood.

◊ Ask lots of questions, especially if you're nervous.

◊ Plant seeds not weeds about yourself. Drop the just.

◊ Talk about things you are passionate about and your future dreams.

◊ Speak positively. Make sure you are not speaking critically about anyone or anything, especially past relationships.

◊ Remember that who you are somewhere is who they will believe you are everywhere. You can't stop people from judging you, but you can influence *how* they judge you. Be mindful of how you present yourself.

◊ Equally share the conversation.

◊ Be inspiring.

◊ Keep good eye contact.

◊ Smile!

◊ Remember that you are too smart to dummy down. Don't act needy or clingy. Your date will appreciate and respect you more for your wit, strength, wisdom, intelligence, and independent ability.

◊ Disconnect from your phone, and give the other person your full attention.

◊ Be bold and help him or her understand how you want to be treated.

◊ Keep a little mystery to yourself. Leave the person wanting to learn more about *you*.

◊ Be a good listener.

◊ It's okay to flirt and be playful, but don't be a tease.

◊ Be present and enjoy the moment.

◊ Be your naturally divamazing self!

Rules for the Dating Diva

◊ To date with respect for herself and for the other person

◊ To be in a relationship for the right reasons

◊ To maintain a balance between her romantic relationship and her family and friends

◊ To never treat her partner like a priority if he or she only treats her like an option

◊ To dress attractively and leave a little mystery to the imagination

◊ To always make sure that her date brings out the best in her and doesn't make her second-guess her divaness

◊ To love herself enough that she can be loved by someone else

◊ To be self-assured and stand confidently in her self-worth

◊ To call the shots and not do anything she is uncomfortable with

◊ To stand in her confidence, character, and intelligence— that's what makes her intriguing and sexy

◊ To enjoy the anticipation and not jump to conclusions

◊ To ask questions if she wants answers

◊ To practice positivity

◊ To be inquisitive—it's a great way to let someone know that she is interested in him or her

◊ To never play mind games—it doesn't say anything good about her character. She treats her partner with the same respect she wants from him or her.

◊ To have fun and enjoy the adventures!

Preparing for and Dealing with Breakups

Nobody treats you better than you treat yourself.
That's so diva!

—Diva

Oh, diva, breakups are hard! In most cases, they hurt and can leave you wondering, *What's wrong with me?* or *What did I do to make (him or her) dump me?* It's normal and understandable to feel that way. And even though it's easy to second-guess yourself and think that you must have done something wrong, don't make it entirely about you. There is nothing wrong with you! Okay, get comfy; grab a box of tissues and a tub of your favorite ice cream, a bag of chips, your favorite chocolate, or whatever your go-to comfort food is; and let's chat.

I'm going to go slightly off course for a quick minute. For everything you do in life, you always should begin with the end in mind. Have a clear picture of what it is you want, the way you want to feel when you achieve it, and the impact or impression you want to make for others. The best way to do that when dating is to consider how you want to be thought of or spoken about if and when you break up. Does this make sense? If you break up with your partner and he or she were to attach a label to you to describe the dating experience with you, what do you want that label to be? Cool? Fun? Inspiring? Those are some favorites. Less appealing labels could be easy, slutty, stupid, bitchy, demanding, and a load to carry. So think about it. How do you want partners to talk about their experience with you? By the way, as a general rule labels don't serve a purpose, so please don't get into a habit of using them at all. However, in this case, it will serve a purpose. It will help you set the tone for the way you want to be perceived, and, in the end, it will help comfort you to know that it might not be about you at all because you showed up at your intended best.

See how powerful this is? When you show up with intention in your life and begin with the end in mind, you have an awful lot of control over the outcome. The true outcome is really about the way you want to feel about yourself even in the midst of sadness, regardless of the result. Another important outcome is you will know a bit more about yourself, what you want, and you don't want in your next relationship.

Now, if you are reading this after you have already experienced a breakup, let's dig into that comfort food and pull up some of those tissues. I never let any teen diva cry alone in my presence. Breakups really do stink, and sometimes there is nothing better than having a good cry to start the healing. The worst thing about breakups is they can cause us to revert to feeling insecure about ourselves, whether it's our character, intelligence, bodies, or overall self-worth. Breakups can make us feel that somehow we weren't good enough and send us on a mad mission to change ourselves, so we don't get hurt again. But have you considered other possibilities? Perhaps your partner had insecurities about measuring up to you. Maybe he or she felt out of your league. Maybe you didn't have enough in common to keep the relationship going. Maybe your schedules conflicted so regularly that it was hard to have a good relationship.

My question for you is why are you taking all of the responsibility for the breakup? You see, you were only able to control half of your relationship—*your half*. If you can only control half of the relationship, why are you taking on the belief and assumption that you are 100 percent responsible for the relationship's collapse and feel that it's your job to change for someone else? You are not a one-size-fits-all human being, and the next person you date might be a better fit for you. If you do want to make changes, make them because you learned a lesson from your experience and want to better yourself, not because someone else made you feel insignificant. There is someone out there who is smart enough to know your value and wonderful enough to treat you well and regularly remind you of your worth.

Try these diva tips to get through a breakup:
- ◊ Surround yourself with the people who know you and make you feel your best.
- ◊ Curl up with your journal and get it all out.
- ◊ Allow yourself to have a good cry when you need it— it's cleansing.
- ◊ Do something to pamper yourself. Perhaps take a bubble bath, get your nails done, or go for a nice long walk.
- ◊ Read an inspiring book or watch your favorite movie.
- ◊ Treat yourself to a sassy new outfit.
- ◊ Be gentle with yourself. It's okay to take the time you need to get through it. We all heal in our own ways and in our own time. Make sure you are not choosing to remain stuck

in grief until the next relationship comes along. Happiness is waiting for you and accessible when you are ready.

◊   Use this power phrase: "Nobody treats me better than I treat myself."

Journal It!

Write about all that you are feeling about the breakup. Pour out your heart on paper. Write about what you learned about yourself, what you want, and you don't want.

Dantra

I know I am worthy of relationships that are healthy and add value to my life. I deserve to feel totally comfortable fully being my diva self in a relationship.

Let it Go!

Let go of the need to blame yourself for what went wrong in your relationship. You can only control your half and cannot possibly be responsible for the entire fallout. Own your part, learn from it, forgive it, and take the lesson with you into your next relationship.

Double Diva Dare Ya!

To be gentle with yourself as you heal your heart. To honor the wonderful young lady you are by doing something good for yourself, reminding yourself of your worth.

Power Tools: Which tools would you use and how would you use them?

- *Assertiveness*
- *Bill of rights*
- *Boundaries*
- *Character*
- *Choices*
- *Compassion*
- *Confidence*
- *Gratitude*
- *Kindness*
- *Language*
- *Ownership*
- *Power phrase*
- *Self-control*
- *Thought and intention*
- *Values*
- *Your voice*

What else will be helpful? _____

D!T DID!:
Ding! This diva is done!

Chapter 7

Online and Personal Safety for the Teen Diva

Don't Put Out There What You Don't Want Out There

The walls of the Internet cannot be washed clean.
Think before you post.

—Diva

Diva, technology is a great thing. It gives us access to endless information. However, it also can be risky because once you put something out there, it can't be taken back. It's out there until the end of time for your family, friends, future relationships, college administrators, employers, and children and grandchildren to see. Can you imagine how much Desdemona loves playing around on the Internet? She stirs up tons of trouble there!

Teenage girls do all kinds of things online. You can tell a teen diva's post from a post by a teenager who is under Desdemona's spell. Teen divas post their successes (without pointing out others' failures or weaknesses), silly pictures, things that empower other teens, jokes that make people laugh, and great things shared about their journey. They are enlightening and encouraging! Desdemona, on the other hand, encourages the girls under her spell to post inappropriate pictures as a way to be liked, to post un-empowering and hateful messages, or to bully online as a way to feel powerful—so *not* diva! Remember, there is *no* power in bullying; it is a sign of poor self-esteem and low confidence.

As you are playing in the world of technology, I want you to counter Desdemona's influence by asking me, your inner diva, a few things first.

Journal It!

- *Why do you want to post or text whatever it is you are considering?*
- *What do you want your post to say about you, your character, and values?*
- *How do you want to make people feel when they read your post or text? Why?*
- *How do you want to feel about your post? Will your post honor those feelings?*
- *What will you gain from this post?*
- *What will you lose from this post?*
- *If you think you will gain attention, why do you feel that you need the attention of that particular peer or group of peers? Is there a better and more empowered way for you to get that attention?*
- *Who are you really doing it for and why?*
- *What are the consequences of this post? What might happen?*

- *Whom will this post affect? In what ways?*
- *What will your post potentially cost you now, a year from now, or five years from now?*
- *Will this post bring you trouble and embarrassment or possibilities for success and good relationships? How?*
- *What does this post really reveal about you, your values, how you see yourself, and your perception of how others see you?*
- *What can you post that will not hurt you or anyone else? Something that empowers others to be their best. Something that says you are* so diva!

Dantra

I will not be influenced by Desdemona or any of her monkeys on the Internet playground. I will choose to inspire and share, and never bully, complain, or condemn. Who I am somewhere is who people will believe me to be everywhere, and I am a diva in all places, setting the example of positivity and peace. I am *a diva pillar of peace!*

Let it Go!

Let go of the need to prove anything to anyone by acting irresponsibly or engaging in cruel activity on the Internet. Be true to your awesome diva character!

Double Diva Dare Ya!

- *To post one thing every day that says something good about you.*
- *To post one thing every day about someone you feel might need a dose of kindness and encouragement. Pay a simple compliment.*

Power Tools: Which tools would you use and how would you use them?

- *Boundaries*
- *Character*
- *Choices*
- *Confidence*
- *Gratitude*
- *Kindness*
- *Language*
- *Thought and intention*
- *Values*

What else will be helpful? _____

DPOP:
Diva pillar of peace

Stranger Danger and Social Media

Don't seek the attention and admiration of strangers.
They are stranger than you think!

—Diva

Growing up, you probably learned and repeatedly heard, "Don't talk to strangers!" and you were educated about the dangers. In today's world, many of these strangers hide behind social media screens. They hide behind these screens so they can be anyone they want to be and look however they want to look. They create fake profiles using made-up personas to look attractive, charming, funny, and smart. It's almost like dressing up for Halloween or some big theatrical production except when the Internet mask is removed, it's not only scary but a real-life nightmare.

If this disturbs you, I will not apologize. I'm here to protect you and keep you safe, so I want you to be educated. There are many kinds of online predators, ranging from sexual predators to human traffickers to child pornographers. Another form of online predator is the bully. Regardless, they are all great performers playing captivating roles with one thing in common: They want to hurt you. Even though some may say things that make you think they care, they don't. The only thing they care about is fulfilling their own sick needs.

Most online predators have an insatiable appetite for portraying themselves as heroes in a young girl's life. With all of the pressures during these years, girls easily fall into the traps of these predators who seemingly swoop in to make things better for them. However, sweet diva, trust me when I tell you that the ending won't be happily ever after. Rather than being a princess swept away and saved from the trials of life, you will wind up being the victim. I won't share horror stories with you about girls who have been victimized by online predators, but you can certainly Google them, and hopefully, you will think twice before engaging with strangers online.

So why do girls start conversations with strangers online? Well, there are many reasons, but in most cases, it all comes down to one common thread: self-esteem. When girls don't feel good about themselves or lack confidence in their ability to be the person they want to be, it can feel refreshing to get a compliment from anyone who makes them feel like a princess and says just the right thing that they need to hear. Some girls do it because they want something they don't have. Perhaps they want a boyfriend because all of their friends have boyfriends. Perhaps they don't feel attractive and need validation that they are beautiful. Online predators are masters at filling the holes of emptiness in a teenage girl's heart. They make girls think, *Wow, finally someone cares and really gets me!*

I want you to understand that a perfect stranger who has never known you couldn't possibly "get you," and there are better and safer ways of filling the emptiness you might be feeling inside. The only people who genuinely get you are those who know and support you and are walking your journey with you. They are the ones you can count on to lift your spirits when you are low and also celebrate your successes. They are the ones who are present *in your life* and not hiding behind masks and screens.

Follow these online safety tips for the teen diva:

◊ *Never* post your personal information! This means your address, phone number, email address, parents' and siblings' names, or anything. If you do this, online predators know where to find you. The bullies in your life will know where to find you. *Anyone* will know where to find you. This not only puts you at risk but it also puts your loved ones at risk.

◊ *Never* agree to meet someone alone you don't know, even if you've been talking to them in a chat room for a long time. You really don't know them, and they don't know you. They may seem nice in the chat space, but their only motive is to build enough trust in you so you will agree to meet them. Then you are in a very dangerous situation.

◊ *Always* get a trusted adult involved if someone pressures you to meet or say/do inappropriate things that make you uncomfortable. Together with that trusted adult, report it. By doing this, you are not only saving yourself but also potentially someone else from getting hurt.

◊ *Never* post pictures of yourself to strangers online. If you do, they will know exactly who you are and what to look for if they decide to stalk you. Make your accounts private.

Journal It!

- *What attracts you to interact with a stranger you met online?*
- *What are the risks you are taking by interacting with this person?*
- *What need is this person fulfilling in you?*
- *What are some other safe ways of having your needs fulfilled?*
- *Who do you know that can support you in fulfilling your needs—and is truly in your life?*

Dantra

Nobody "gets" me better than the people who truly care about me and are walking with me on my journey. I will not interact with strangers online and make myself vulnerable to danger. My self-worth is greater!

Let it Go!

Let go of the need to reach out to strangers in order to feel good about yourself. Instead, choose to spend time with friends who remind you of your greatness.

Double Diva Dare Ya!

To stop engaging with strangers online! If you or your friends are engaging with online strangers, report those who ask for pictures of any nature, especially inappropriate photos, or pressure you to meet. Do this for yourself, and do it for your friends. We divas have to stand up for each other and protect each other.

Power Tools: Which tools would you use and how would you use them?

- *Boundaries*
- *Choices*
- *Confidence*
- *Language*
- *Power phrase*
- *Thought and intention*
- *Your voice*

What else will be helpful? _____

Chapter 8

Other Life Skills and Bonus Content for the Teen Diva

Simple Etiquette for the Teen Diva

◊ When someone smiles at you, smile back.

◊ When someone says, "Hi! How are you?" be courteous and return the question. You have no idea how much it means and what this simple courtesy says about you as a person.

◊ Make a difference in someone's day by paying a random compliment or offering a word of encouragement.

◊ Always acknowledge people who speak to you, text you, and do nice things for you.

◊ Accept a compliment with a polite "thank you."

◊ Congratulate others when they win.

◊ Keep your commitments.

◊ Send a handwritten thank-you note.

◊ Take a minute to show you care.

◊ Unplug from technology, and be present in a conversation.

◊ Say please and thank you.

◊ Don't leave people hanging.

◊ Accept a gift graciously with heartfelt thanks.

◊ Take care of your personal hygiene.

◊ Be inquisitive and show interest in others.

◊ Don't show up empty-handed; bring a gift or a card to show your appreciation.

◊ Teach but also be teachable.

◊ Keep your promises.

◊ Practice non-judgment.

◊ Be a good listener.

◊ Watch your language.

◊ Be humble.

◊ Be love.

◊ Most importantly, *always be kind!*

Money Management for the Teen Diva

Money is a tool that if used wisely today will help you create the dreams for your tomorrow.

—Diva

You already might be working a part-time job, or you may be anticipating working and earning your own money in the near future. Whatever income you receive now or in the future, always pay yourself first. You might think that you're only a teenager now, so saving isn't something you need to worry about yet, but honestly, you can never start too soon—and saving money is a great way to feel good about yourself. It's also a great exercise in practicing independence while you still have support.

You've read an awful lot of information throughout this book about creating your own story without influence and the power tool of choice in all we experience. Consider money management as a tool that you will use in creating your future story tomorrow, next year, five years from now, and throughout your life. Money is a necessary part of that story regardless of whether your goal is to have an unlimited supply of it or to live simply. Either way, you will need it. The cool thing is that right now you have a safety net and a great opportunity to take advantage of getting a jump start on saving. You don't have any bills to pay or financial commitments to meet. Your job as a teenager is to study, learn, and grow into the divamazing lady you are meant to be.

The adults in your life will not be around forever to provide everything you want. You will eventually have to stand on your own two feet and earn what you want in life. The more prepared you are, the less it will feel like a struggle when you do reach full independence. And here's the thing: You will never fully appreciate what you have until you have honestly earned it, and there is no greater feeling than how you feel once you have done it on your own. People will also respect you more and be more inspired by you for having done it on your own, even if it was the hard way.

Money management is a powerful exercise in being responsible and fully owning your life and living it well.

Diva Tips for Money Management:

◊ Always pay yourself first by putting twenty percent of what you earn into a savings account that you will never touch.

◊ Always pay yourself first by putting money for your future goals into another account. For example, if you want to buy a car when you are sixteen years old, take a trip with friends, buy a ski pass, or whatever you desire, figure out how much money you need to save and put it in a special account. You will feel awesome for having accomplished those goals on your own!

◊ Divas make the world a better and brighter place. We are all about helping others. Do what you wish, but I also encourage you to remember those less fortunate and be charitable with a portion of your income. I recommend ten percent, but it's your call. Any help you give makes a big difference! That good karma will come back to you tenfold.

◊ Make sure you budget and keep money out for your own fun and enjoyment. Every diva needs to have fun!

◊ **Warning:** Desdemona might influence your ability to be financially responsible by telling you that you can put something on a credit card and pay it over time. What she isn't telling you is that for every dollar you put on a credit card, the credit card company (after interest and special fees) takes up to twenty-five percent. That's a lot of money! The other thing is if you can't pay it back or miss payments because you can't afford them, it damages your credit rating and limits what you will be able to do in your future. Don't fall into Desdemona's trap. Remember to not spend what you don't have.

Journal It!

*Let's begin with the end in mind. Well, not the "very end,"
but let's say later in life:*

- *What do you want retirement to look like?*
- *When you are fifty years old, what do you want to have accomplished? What do you want your lifestyle to be?*
- *When you are forty years old, what do you want to have accomplished? What will your life look like, and what do you need to attain your ideal life by forty?*
- *When you are thirty years old, what do you want to have accomplished? What will your life look like and what do you need to attain your ideal life by thirty?*
- *When you graduate from college, what do you want your life to look like? Where do you want to live? What do you want to learn next?*
- *How much money will you need to live and begin creating your independent life?*

Dantra

*Money management and responsibility are a part of my
story. How I manage my money now will determine how
I write my future story.*

Let it Go!

*Let go of spending what you don't have. Instead, save up
for your desires. You'll feel really good about yourself and
what you've accomplished.*

Power Tools: Which tools would you use and how would you use them?

- *Assertiveness*
- *Choices*
- *Confidence*
- *Gratitude*
- *Ownership*
- *Power phrase*
- *Values*

What else will be helpful? _____

Empowering Conversation Starters for the Teen Diva

◊ How do you choose gifts for your friends?

◊ How do you define success for yourself?

◊ How would you describe your ideal day?

◊ If I, your inner diva, gave you three wishes, what would they be?

◊ If you and your friends came together to create a character or superhero, what would that character be? Name it. Describe the personality. Say what this character would *divaly* accomplish.

◊ If you could solve one big problem at your school, what would it be?

◊ If you woke up tomorrow as a superhero what would your powers be and what would you do with them?

◊ If you woke up tomorrow and something you wanted changed for you, what would it be and what about you made it happen?

◊ In what ways can you step up and change the life of someone who is struggling, someone you wouldn't normally hang out with?

◊ In what ways do you exercise playfulness?

◊ Name a goal you have this year. How will you reward yourself when you achieve it?

◊ No one treats you better than you treat yourself. What do you do to pamper yourself?

◊ What are all of the unique gifts of the divas in this conversation? How do you come together to support each other using your unique gifts?

◊ What are you doing when you are happiest and honoring me, your inner diva, in your bliss?

◊ What are you doing when you feel like your truest self?

◊ What are you looking most forward to?

◊ What are you most grateful for?

◊ What are you most proud of in your life?

◊ What are your favorite parts of yourself?

◊ What are your greatest gifts and talents?

◊ What are your top five *must-haves* in a dating partner?

◊ What can you do to stretch yourself and exercise more confidence?

◊ What can you do to use your diva gifts and help someone or solve a problem today?

◊ What character do you most admire and why?

◊ What did you learn today that will lead you to a brighter diva future tomorrow?

◊ What do you do to pamper yourself like a diva?

◊ What memory brings you great happiness?

◊ What ways do you practice kindness?

◊ What do you know how to do that you can teach others?

◊ What do you love most about yourself?

◊ What gets you super zany excited about life?

◊ What motivates you to be your best?

◊ What makes you feel like a lucky girl?

◊ What can you do to be kinder to yourself?

◊ What do you want less of in your life?

◊ What do you want more of in your life?

◊ What five words would you use to describe yourself at your best?

◊ What five words would your friends use to describe you at your best?

◊ What guides the choices you make?

◊ What have been your greatest successes this year? Who cheered you on and supported you?

◊ What haven't you forgiven and why?

◊ What is the difference you want to make in the world? Why?

◊ What is your best feature?

◊ What is your big vision for your future?

◊ What is your favorite memory from your elementary school days?

◊ What is your favorite thing to do?

◊ What is your ideal first date?

◊ What kind of independence do you look forward to in the future?

◊ What qualities do you look for in a friend? In what ways do you exercise those qualities in yourself?

◊ What talent do you have that most people don't know about?

◊ What would you name your inner diva, and how did you come up with it?

◊ What's an example of something you have learned to forgive?

◊ What's most important to you in the way you want to be treated by friends, family, and romantic partners?

◊ What's the funniest thing that happened this week?

◊ What's the greatest lesson you have learned?

◊ What's your guilty pleasure?

◊ When you are most happy, what are you doing?

◊ Where are you spending time that doesn't feed your diva spirit?

◊ Where would you like to spend more time that will feed your diva spirit?

◊ Which friends would I, your inner diva, like the most? Why?

◊ Who are the people in your life that support you the most? How can you spend more time with them?

◊ Who are you most proud of in your life?

◊ Who is your favorite movie/TV star, and why do you admire him or her?

My Inner Diva

Desdemona, ill-fated one,
You have no power over me.
You can try and try, but when my day is done,
I am at peace because my diva guided me.

She shouts a loud *no*
When you try to take me where I should not go
And pats me on the back for my successes.
The negative ways you have tried to define me
The greatness in me, my diva, one hundred times louder professes.

My diva always has my back
And presents me with a brighter path
Even when you try to shadow me with your darkness.
However, Desdemona, ill-fated one,
I choose to not listen to your harshness.

You clearly don't want what's best for me
Because you only feel alive in your misery.
However, Desdemona, ill-fated one,
I choose to live my life blissfully.

I will not follow you, Desdemona, ill-fated one.
I will not choose you when my day is done.
The diva inside is my ultimate guide
To live a life on the loving and brighter side.

~Diva

The Diva Dictionary

2BHI2HMD!	To be happy is to honor my diva!
BAD	Being a diva
BAD-ASS	Being a diva—amazing, sweet, sassy
BAG	Being a goddess
BITWOD	Balance is the way of the diva
BOYC	Be your own character
BYADC!	Be youniquely and divally captivating
CD4PC	Compassionate divas for positive change
D!TDID	Ding! this diva is done
DANTRA	Diva's mantra
DBOH	Diva badge of honor
DDCR	Dating divas command respect
DDDB	Divas don't do blah
DED	Divas empowering divas
DITCH	Diva in total control of herself
Divafied	Transformed into the amazing diva you are meant to be
Divaly	Done in diva style

Divamazing	Amazing in your unique diva style
Divaness	Unique goddess gifts and style
DLOA	Diva law of attraction
DOW	Diva of the world
DPOP	Diva pillar of peace
DQDRTW	Drama queen dropouts rule the world
DSD	Divas supporting divas
FLMDT	Fearlessly living my diva truth
HDAS	Hot damn and shazam!
IASD	I am so diva
IOK2SINOK	It's okay to say it's not okay
ISGT!	I've so got this!
LLM	Leave a little mystery
MAMIG	Me and my inner goddess
MHAP	Making happiness a priority
MVD	Most valuable diva
MWIMW	My word is my wand
N2DD	Not today, Desdemona
N2DF	Not today, fear

NIACS	No is a complete sentence
OIBMID	Only influenced by my inner diva
OMD!	Oh, my diva!
PADS	Planting a diva seed
SIMDS	Stepping into my diva style
SOD	Sisterhood of divas
UBU	You be you
URSD!	You are so diva!
WTD	What the Desdemona
WWAGD?	What would a goddess do?
WWADD?	What would a diva do?
WYG	Weed your garden

Add your own diva codes

Conclusion

My sweet teen diva, you may have noticed that there are no specific instructions on how to be a certain way or deal with a certain struggle. The reason for this is that what makes you powerful is your creative inner diva, who will guide you in the choices you make and the values attached to those choices when you are faced with a situation. As I have emphasized throughout this book—that it's impossible to live by the definitions society has inflicted on you about what a beautiful and successful teenage girl "should be"—I cannot tell you the best way to handle the situations you will face in life. I can only guide you and provide you with the tools that will empower you to discern what is right for you, so you can create the life you desire in your own diva style.

Should you hit a bump in the road and want some outside guidance or perspective, visit www.ThatsSoDiva.com. There you will find resources and programs that are available to you.

Dare to be *you* and shine your light, diva darling! The best promise you can make to yourself and to me is to love and respect yourself as much as I love and respect you. And ... to never, ever, ever give up!

With all my diva love,

—Diva

Hotlines and Helpful Resources for the Teen Diva

*If you feel threatened and/or are in a life-and-death situation, call **911**.*

Alcohol and Drug Abuse

Al-Anon/Alateen	888-425-2666 https://al-anon.org/newcomers/teen-corner-alateen/
Crisis Call Center	800-273-8255 http://www.crisiscallcenter.org/substance-abuse/
National Alcohol and Substance Abuse Information Center	800-784-6776 http://www.addictioncareoptions.com
Thursday's Child National Youth Advocacy Hotline	800-872-5437 http://www.thursdayschild.org

Bullying

Crisis Call Center	800-273-8255 http://crisiscallcenter.org/crisisservices-html/
Cyber Tipline	800-843-5678 http://www.cybertipline.com

National Suicide Hotline	800-784-2433 http://www.hopeline.com
Thursday's Child National Youth Advocacy Hotline	800-872-5437 http://www.thursdayschild.org
The Trevor Project (LGBT)	866-488-7386 http://www.thetrevorproject.org

Eating Disorders

Crisis Call Center	800-273-8255 http://crisiscallcenter.org/crisisservices-html/
National Association of Anorexia Nervosa and Associated Disorders	630-577-1330 http://www.anad.org
National Eating Disorders Association	800-931-2237 http://www.nationaleatingdisorders.org
Thursday's Child National Youth Advocacy Hotline	800-872-5437 http://www.thursdayschild.org

Grief/Loss

Crisis Call Center	800-273-8255 http://crisiscallcenter.org/crisisservices-html/
National Hopeline Network	800-784-2433 http://www.hopeline.com
Tragedy Assistance Program for Survivors	800-959-8277 http://www.taps.org
Thursday's Child National Youth Advocacy Hotline	800-872-5437 http://www.thursdayschild.org

Homelessness and Runaways

Crisis Call Center	800-273-8255 http://crisiscallcenter.org/crisisservices-html/
Covenant House	800-388-3888 http://www.covenanthouse.org
National Runaway Safeline	800-786-2929 http://www.runaway.org
Thursday's Child National Youth Advocacy Hotline	800-872-5437 http://www.thursdayschild.org

School Violence

Crisis Call Center	800-273-8255 http://crisiscallcenter.org/crisisservices-html/
Safe2Tell	877-542-7233 https://www.safe2tell.org
Speak Up	866-773-2587 http://www.bradycampaign.org
Thursday's Child National Youth Advocacy Hotline	800-872-5437 http://www.thursdayschild.org

Sexual and Domestic Violence

Childhelp USA National Child Abuse Hotline	800-422-4453 https://www.childhelp.org
Crisis Call Center	800-273-8255 http://crisiscallcenter.org/crisisservices-html/
Love Is Respect, National Teen Dating Abuse Helpline	866-331-9474 http://www.loveisrespect.org
National Domestic Violence Hotline	800-799-7233 http://www.ndvh.org

Rape, Abuse, and Incest National Network	800-656-4673 http://www.rainn.org
Thursday's Child National Youth Advocacy Hotline	800-872-5437 http://www.thursdayschild.org

Sexual Health and Sexuality

GLBT National Youth Talkline	800-246-7743 http://www.ginh.org/talkline
Planned Parenthood National Hotline	800-230-7526 http://www.plannedparenthood.org
Trans Lifeline	US: 877-565-8860 Canada: 877-330-6366 http://www.translifeline.org

Suicide

Crisis Call Center	800-273-8255 http://crisiscallcenter.org/crisisservices-html/
National Suicide Hotline	800-784-2433 http://www.hopeline.com
National Suicide Prevention Lifeline	800-273-8255 http://www.suicidepreventionlifeline.org

Thursday's Child National Youth Advocacy Hotline	800-872-5437 http://www.thursdayschild.org

Teen Pregnancy and Parenting

Baby Safe Haven	888-510-2229 http://www.safehaven.tv/states
Postpartum Support International	800-944-4773 http://www.postpartum.net
American Pregnancy Helpline	866-942-6466 http://www.thehelpline.org
Birthright International	800-550-4900 http://www.birthright.org
Crisis Call Center	800-273-8255 http://crisiscallcenter.org/crisisservices-html/
Planned Parenthood National Hotline	800-230-7526 http://www.plannedparenthood.org
Thursday's Child National Youth Advocacy Hotline	800-872-5437 http://www.thursdayschild.org

References

Achor, Shawn. *The happiness advantage.* New York: Crown Publishing Group, 2010.

Brown, Brene. *Daring greatly.* New York: Avery, 2012

Carnegie, Dale. *How to win friends and influence people.* New York: Pocket Books, 1964

Costin, Carolyn. & Schubert Grabb, Gwen. *8 Keys to recovery from an eating disorder.* New York: W.W. Norton & Company, Inc., 2012

Goddess Guide. http://www.goddessguide.com. (2007-2019).

Hanson, Rick. & Mendius, Richard. *Buddha's brain.* Oakland, CA: New Harbinger Publications, Inc, 2009

Hay, Louise. *The power is within you.* New York: Hay House, Inc., 1991.

Helmstetter, Shad. T*he power of neuro-plasticity.* Gulf Breeze, FL: Park Avenue Press, 2013

Horn, Sam. *Take the bully by the horns.* New York: St. Martin's Press, 2002

Jensen, Diane Mastromarino. *The girls guide to loving yourself* Boulder, CO: Blue Mountain Arts, Inc. 2003

Johnson, Chalene. http://www.getcourageousconfidence.com (2017)

Kay, Katty. & Shipman, Claire. *The confidence code for girls.* New York: HarperCollins Publishers, 2018

Leaf, Caroline. *Think learn succeed.* Grand Rapids, MI: Baker Books, 2018

Lipton, Bruce. *The biology of belief.* Carlsbad, CA: Hay House, Inc., 2005

Lowndes, Leil. *How to be a people magnet.* Chicago, IL: Contemporary Books, 2001

Maxwell, John. *Sometimes you win sometimes you learn.* New York: Hachette Book Group, 2015.

McWilliams, Peter. *Love 101.* Los Angeles, CA: Prelude Press, 1995

Schab, Lisa. *The self-esteem workbook for teens.* Oakland, CA: Instant Help Books, 2013

Schneider, Bruce. *Energy leadership.* Hoboken, NJ: John Wiley & Sons, Inc., 2008

Acknowledgments

Inspiration for this book came from many different relationships, experiences, and conversations. Every friend and family member inspired this book in some way and helped me to develop and embrace my inner diva over the course of my life. I am overflowing with gratitude for all of you and the joy you have brought into my life. Thank you!

This book wouldn't have been possible without the contributions, guidance, efforts, and support of some key individuals.

First and most importantly, I want to thank my parents for their unfailing support and encouragement throughout my entire life. You have shown me what it means to love unconditionally and live with integrity. You grounded me in my faith, and also showed me the importance of believing in myself and my dreams. It is a privilege and a blessing to be your daughter.

To Ali Romley, I am so proud and honored to have had you contribute your gifts to this book. Not only are you a talented artist who put together a beautiful cover design; you continually inspire me with your confidence, kindness, compassion, strength, and your radiant light that you shine for this world. You are *so* diva!

To Kirsten Jensen at My Word Publishing, it's rare to meet people who live with such integrity in all that they do and who are as genuine, kind, and caring as you. You saved my book, brought this project back to life and walked with me on my journey to make this dream a reality. There are not enough words to express my deepest and most heartfelt gratitude. I am on bended knee and will never forget all you have done for me!

To my dear friend Kathy Hendricks, you've been such an inspiration to me through your writings, your programs, and all that you do to empower women and families to stay grounded, balanced, and connected in their faith. You are the example of living a purpose-filled life with and in grace. Thank you for your guidance, your belief in me, your encouragement, your generosity of time, and most of all, your precious friendship.

To Debra King, thank you for the friendship we share and being my mentor in so many ways over the years. You sparked me to write this book with one single conversation and cheered me on through the process. You have added so much richness to my life through your spirit, strength, and loving and supportive presence.

Many thanks to Shauna Kalicki and Paula Evans, two dear friends who are examples of stepping into and owning who they are and using their loving hearts, wisdom, and gift of playfulness to shine a light in this world.

To my friend Janine Phillips, who has walked this road of life with me since we were young teenagers. You are a treasure! You supported me throughout this entire journey, cheering me on, and never doubting that I would someday publish my book. Your strength, beauty, wisdom, and the experiences we have shared since we were teens inspired me more than you will ever know. You have always been, continue to be, and always will be a rock in my life. You are *so* diva in every way my precious, friend.

To my dear friend, Kevin. You are such a ray of light in my life. Thank you for your encouragement, every conversation, your witty sense of humor, and your thoughtful and wise perspectives.

The quality of a book is largely dependent on the quality of the editor. Jennifer Bisbing, it was an honor having someone of your caliber work on this book. You have a beautiful spirit and an energetic enthusiasm for your work – that's SO diva! Thank you for your professionalism, thoughtfulness, and your attention to every last detail.

Brianne Smith, you are such a bright light and that light was reflected in the quality of your work on the interior design of this book. You beautifully matched the positivity that I want to inspire in my readers. It has been a pleasure working with you!

About the Author

Andrea Spoor, the author of *That's So Diva! A Teen Girl's Guide to Loving Herself and Living Beautifully*, is a certified professional coach, speaker, and leader of empowerment programs for teenage girls. Andrea helps girls gain clarity from the confusion, challenges, chaos, and pressures of the teenage years by introducing them to their inner Diva, so they can move forward confidently and assured in their futures. Andrea believes that every girl is born a diva with unique gifts, her own brand of beauty, a special inner strength, a captivating spirit, and endless opportunities. For more information or to contact Andrea for speaking engagements or book clubs, visit www.AndreaSpoor.com.

* 9 7 8 1 7 3 2 9 7 9 3 0 7 *